THOMAS MERTON

The Springs of
Contemplation

The Lamb will guide them to the springs of the water of life.

Revelation 7:17

THOMAS MERTON

A Retreat at the Abbey of Gethsemani

The Springs of Contemplation

Foreword by

Kathleen Norris

author of *The Cloister Walk*

AVE MARIA PRESS
Notre Dame, Indiana 46556

#35849069

Library of Congress Cataloging-in-Publication Data

Merton, Thomas, 1915-1968.
    The springs of contemplation : a retreat at the Abbey of
Gethsemani / Thomas Merton ; edited by Jane Marie
Richardson.
            p.   cm.
    Originally published : New York : Farrar, Straus, Giroux,
c1992.
    ISBN 0-87793-598-X
    1. Retreats for members of religious orders. 2. Monastic
and religious life. 3. Monasticism and religious orders for
women. 4. Contemplative orders. 5. Abbesses, Christian—
Religious life. 6. Spiritual life—Catholic Church. 7.
Contemplation. 8. Catholic Church—Doctrines. I.
Richardson, Jane Marie.   II. Title.
    [BX4214.M47   1997]
    269'.6943—dc21
                                                96-47761
                                                CIP

Contents

Foreword

I find it refreshing, when reading this roughcut gem of a book, to find that back in the late 1960s, as Thomas Merton wrestled with what it could mean for monastic people to be prophetic in the world, he was himself being prophetic, saying what we need to hear now, at the close of this chaotic century. As we drown in the verbiage of advertising it helps to be reminded that "People don't want to hear any more words. In our mechanical age, all words have become alike. . . . To say 'God is Love' is like saying, 'Eat Wheaties.'"

Merton reveals a considerable prescience with regard to the way in which a celebrity culture comes to trivialize everything. A glance at any magazine rack confirms his observation that "everything is reduced to a kind of indifference. . . . Page 1 is a nun with a new habit, page 2 is a burlesque queen—equally newsworthy. There's no indication that one thing means more than another." In a way, *Springs of Contemplation* is as much about American consumerism as it is about American monastic life in the era just after Vatican II.

I treasure the way that Merton makes us aware of the extent to which we have been formed as consumers; the extent to which in a society "organized for profit and for marketing . . . there's no freedom. You're free to choose your gimmicks, your brand of TV, your make of new car. But you're not free not to have a car." To be prophetic now, Merton tells the contemplative nuns he'd invited to Gethsemani, is to begin to speak like the Old Testament prophets, "telling people who think they're free that they're slaves."

Freedom, of course, was a buzzword of the 1960s, and Merton recognized even in the midst of that heady decade that the merely novel was often being mistaken for the prophetic, and that seemingly countercultural movements such as the hippies were in fact a part of the mainstream. In several passages Merton suggests that both contemporary industrial society and the Roman Catholic church are structured to allow for quantitative rather than qualitative change. And he firmly claims (or reclaims) Christian monasticism as a resistance movement standing for the latter.

As a window into the lives of contemplative nuns in mid-century, this book provides occasion for reflection on how much (and how little) has changed in the past thirty years. The questions the sisters bring up—should contemplative nuns be given permission to have sisters in active apostolates take retreats with them? Should nuns be allowed to read *Time?*—are of their era. And Merton's responses are a treasure—in the first case, why ask permission, why not simply do it? "If you love someone, you invite them in," he says. As to the second question: yes, "if you're asking if nuns should be informed"; no "if it implies that by reading *Time* you are informed."

At a time when books such as *One-Minute Wisdom* fill bookstore shelves, it's good to hear Merton say, "There's no such thing as a quick course in contemplation. It just doesn't exist. If it does, somebody's being sold a bill of goods." As meditation, spiritual direction, and traditional monastic prayer become increasingly popular among lay people, including many outside the churches, it is good to keep in mind Merton's view that for all such practices, "self-forgetfulness is the real litmus test."

Springs of Contemplation is of its time, but it is also strikingly contemporary. Merton says, for instance, that both Zen and Christian monasticism are for ordinary life, ordinary people. He points out that in a Christianity centered on the incarnation, "theology . . . happens in relations between people" and that "because we love, God is present." In his hope that monasteries might be truly countercultural, he says to the women, "We're supposed to provide a place where people can find what they can't find elsewhere."

With monastic vocations to contemplative houses on the rise, and retreat facilities booked for many months in advance, it would seem that contemporary monasteries are doing just that.

Kathleen Norris

Introduction

Thomas Merton, our friend and neighbor in rural Kentucky, wrote me in the fall of 1967: "I'd like to invite you to a little gathering of contemplative sisters (prioresses, really), which I am planning for early December. They need my help. You are invited to attend the conferences, and maybe you can assist in transportation and in welcoming them."

I was delighted to help and it was a marvelous opportunity to be present at several of the sessions of the little retreat. The same invitation was issued again in May 1968, and once more I had the privilege of sharing Merton's insights with twelve or more contemplative prioresses from their respective communities.

In that time of incredibly swift changes in our world and in the post-Vatican II Church, Merton saw the need of assisting contemplatives who were often cut off by inflexible regulations—for example, in travel and reading—from any analysis of important movements taking place in the Church and world. Merton knew that, as a widely recognized leader in prayer and contemplative life, he had our confidence. He saw that he could serve as mentor or catalyst in a needed development. Also, I knew that he had tried in other ways, such as by letters and visits to authorities, to accomplish this humanizing goal, and had not succeeded. In various ways, especially through correspondence, Merton had come to know and value many of these contemplative prioresses and to understand what was happening in their lives. Now he would be able to meet them in person and conduct a dialogue with them face-to-face.

Merton sought no permissions to hold such a meeting,

nor did the sisters, to attend it. His own abbot graciously extended the hospitality of the guest house and grounds at the Abbey of Gethsemani for the sessions. The beautiful and restful setting of the monastery in Kentucky encouraged and enhanced the camaraderie which readily sprang up among the participants. We often sat on the banks of one of the lakes or ponds, which Merton delighted in showing us, places which have become familiar landmarks to his many readers. I recall his taking us (the retreatants) up the back hill to see his hard-earned hermitage. With obvious pleasure, he showed us all his little treasures, including bongo drums given him by a friend, a stole sent to him by John XXIII, and various relics that he cherished. I remember writing him from Rome, asking if he would like a first-class relic of the newly canonized Lebanese hermit, Charbel. "Oh yes," he answered, "I'm a great relic man!"

Merton believed in the faith reality lived by contemplative women. He realized that their vocations demanded a new maturity within a patriarchal system. Because I had only recently come back from Vatican II as an observer ("auditor," in official terms), Merton was glad to have me affirm, through my experience, some of his own thinking about the unwillingness of Curia members to listen to the experience of American women. "You have to believe in yourselves, your life, and not be dissuaded from your own convictions," he said. As often as I could, I consulted him about changes in the Church, expressing, too, my puzzlement in dealing with some Vatican II documents which offered opposing directions, sometimes in the same document. "Take what you want," he said abruptly, "as long as it's there."

Merton was a good teacher, as his former monastic students are quick to affirm. In these talks to us, Merton's skill at communicating showed itself in his ability to open up to us new ways of seeing and new hopes for our human and religious lives. He was equally capable of listening attentively to our questions and comments, taking seriously what was offered with neither condescension nor passive acceptance. He had a knack for crediting others, thus eliciting their best efforts. Ever witty, ever exuding life, Merton fired our deepest desires.

For me, there has always been a clarity and firmness in Merton's approach to problems; not that he glossed over the difficulties, of which there were plenty in these changing times, but he had the sureness of his own exploration and conclusions to recommend to others.

In preparation for the conference, Merton sent some questions for the participants to ponder. Perhaps the most telling one was "What would you do if organized religious life were to disappear?" The relevance of exploring such a question illustrates Merton's talent for cutting through non-essentials, and engaging the mind and heart directly. Merton did not pretend to have answers; he knew that was not his task. Nor did he have an opportunity to correct or enlarge upon ideas presented in the retreat. But fertile seeds are there.

As the meeting progressed, I could see themes emerging which Merton was to emphasize in the writing of his last days: "Stand on your own two feet." "Give courage to the creative and imaginative new members who need a compassionate community." "Proceed to live your life as you think you must." Merton's proclamation of authentic autonomy, the overcoming of alienation, permeates the comments contained in these pages. He communicated strongly his own belief in the value of the contemplative life in general, and of the lives of these sisters in particular, and he underlined this conviction with fresh insight for all of us.

I have a lasting impression of Merton's welcoming warmth and ease of manner, which delighted all of us and created an atmosphere of good humor throughout the few days of each gathering. Meals and free times were sources of growing companionship in a climate of open exchange. Merton didn't know how to be stiff or formal with others, and his ability to be a friendly resource filled these days with special enjoyment. There were walks in the woods and coffee breaks. Later, Merton commented in letters how much he appreciated this time with the sisters.

Since these conferences—these "non-workshops," as

Merton merrily designated them—I have often considered the value of getting their contents in print. Finally, a few years ago, I secured a complete set of the tapes from Sister Elaine Bane, the Allegheny Franciscan sister present at the meetings, who herself provided much of the impetus for these gatherings. Then I asked Sister Cecily Jones, S.L., to type up a transcript from these tapes. Every word! No small task, that, but absolutely essential to the whole project. Arline Newton, a Merton scholar, also had a hand in typing the tapes.

Then I asked Sister Jane Marie Richardson, S.L., who went with me to some of the conferences, to do the final editing. She accomplished this task with clarity and skill, and with great faithfulness to the text. I think Merton—as an editor himself—would be highly pleased.

Readers will note in the chapter headings the wide range of topics covered by Merton in these few days. A sampling includes such themes as "Community of Love," "Prophetic Choices," "Contemplative Reality and the Living Christ." One topic which I am sure will be of particular interest is Merton's discussion of "The Feminine Mystique." Ever alive to new and growing aspects of true autonomy, Merton read eagerly the writings of Simone de Beauvoir, Betty Friedan, and Mary Daly. His quick mind grasped the critique presented by these women, and he supported their awareness of women's oppression.

Although these gatherings were purposefully casual, intended to put everyone at ease, they were also purposefully serious because of the profound nature of the topics treated. Readers will probably find in these conferences a substantial resource for their own lives. So well did Merton discern—nearly twenty-five years ago—the impact of culture and events on our times that I believe we have not caught up with him yet.

Here, speaking to this little group of nuns, is a great spiritual leader, compassionate and gifted, sharing his own vision with all of us, intelligently and with love.

Sister Mary Luke Tobin, S. L.

Editor's Note

In editing the recordings of the two retreats, we have been as faithful as possible to the thought, style, and spirit of our brother Tom. The text was not, of course, written, but was spoken by him. We felt we owed him the usual editorial courtesies, knowing he would not like us to leave participles dangling, infinitives split, and so on.

Special thanks are due to Sisters Mary Luke Tobin, Cecily Jones, and Mary Swain of Loretto, as well as to Monsignor William Shannon of Nazareth College, Rochester, and Brother Patrick Hart of the Abbey of Gethsemani in the preparation and editing of the retreat. In a few cases proper names have been supplied for persons referred to by Merton. The passages in italics indicate questions and comments made by the retreatants. The initials "S.L." refer to the Sisters of Loretto, a religious community of women founded in Kentucky in 1812. An essay Thomas Merton wrote on the 150th anniversary of the order, "Loretto and Gethsemani," appears as an appendix to this book.

Sister Jane Marie Richardson, S.L.

PART ONE

Abbey

—— OF ——

Gethsemani

DECEMBER 1967

Presence, Silence, Communication

In the contemplative life we all face the question "What are we supposed to do?" One thing we can do is come together like this, as sisters and brothers in Christ, and let happen what has not happened before, this kind of searching retreat.

Certainly what we are doing now is what we're supposed to do: getting together in a quiet place, where we can talk and think and pray. An important key word is *presence*. We want to be present to each other and then trust what happens. If you've just read my books, you don't really know me, so you better get a look at the real thing. Presence is what counts. It's important to realize that the Church itself is presence, and so is the contemplative life. Community is presence, not an institution. We've been banking on the ability to substitute institution for the reality of presence, and it simply won't work.

There is a kind of Pentecost in miniature wherever there is Church. Pentecost means "new life," and that means changes in our lives. But changes are not easy; new life is disturbing. The basic experience of religious in our time has been the struggle of knowing in their hearts that something is asked of them by God and yet somehow they are being prevented from doing it. It is true that a lot of young people who come to religious life feel they have to leave it in order to find God. For some this is probably true, even though for others it may be an illusion. All of us are trying to sort out things about our lives. It's going to take a long time; the answers are not there.

Take the question of silence, for example, our specialty

here at a Trappist monastery. Silence can be a great problem or a great grace. When it becomes too formalized, it ceases to be a source of grace and becomes a problem because it is no longer a helping presence. For too long the rule of silence was a means of being absent from one another. This sets up a contradiction, and people suffer from it. A community can't exist on those terms. Contradictions are a part of life, but systematic frustration of cultural values is another matter. A person has to be able to get along without a lot of distracting things in the culture, naturally, but that doesn't mean we should never be able to hear a symphony. We Trappists have a bad reputation for that kind of thing. Our silence tended to operate in that mechanical way. Also silence almost meant you had to pretend that no one else was present. You were silent because you were more or less excluding people.

When people come together, there is always some kind of presence, even the kind that can give a person an ulcer. What we have to do is arrange things in such a way that the presence is a positive and not a negative experience. This means we may have to talk more in order to learn how to be present in silence in a positive way. There has to be enough communication so that silence can be a grace. That kind of silence demands a deeper love, and until that much love is developed, there's no point in pretending that the love is there when it isn't. The justification of silence in our life is that we love one another enough to be silent together. Once we get into the depths of community life, we realize that there is a very special duty and grace in being silent together, but we don't arrive at this by excluding others or treating them as objects. It happens gradually as we learn to love.

A friend of mine, a Dutch psychoanalyst [Joost A. Merloo], has a very fine manuscript on silence. He points out that we have to keep readjusting our understanding and practice of silence so that it can remain a definite value. We recognize that we have been misusing it, but we see also that we need to keep it for its real value, we need to renew it. We renew our silence, not by going around talking to people endlessly or by giving up our way of life, but by letting the quiet be impregnated with presence and with light. Then it's life-giving.

Our being is silent, but our existence is noisy. Our actions tend to be noisy, but when they stop, there is a ground of silence which is always there. Our job as contemplatives is to be in contact with that ground and to communicate from that level, and not just to be in contact with a stream of activities which are constantly moving. We have to keep silence alive for other people, as well as for ourselves—because no one else is doing it. We may think people don't care about this, but in fact they care about it very much. Silence is greatly symbolic in our time. Even though there's talk about contemplative life and its values not making much sense to people today, or not being of much interest to them, this is not true. Many people are looking to contemplation and meditation for meaning. You've heard of the Beatles, I'm sure. What are they doing now [in 1967]? They are seeing a yogi for instruction in meditation.

The world is full of people who are looking for meditation and silence, and most of them are not Catholic. This is true in Russia and in the Iron Curtain countries. We had a postulant here, a Hungarian refugee, who was a seminarian. A friend of his, a Communist in Yugoslavia, an engineer and a world chess champion, had been brought up with no religion whatever. But he was assiduously practicing yoga because he felt the need of some kind of interior silence. Probably the biggest religious revival in the world is going to happen in Russia, because Russian scientists are very interested in the question of religion and God, much more so than a lot of people in Christian countries.

In other words, people recognize these values; they know such values ought to be. Time and again people come here, often of no particular faith, who are sensitive to the fact that here is a place of silence and a place, presumably, where silence is understood and valued. Therefore, it is terribly important for us to be clear about our silence. The last thing we should do is get rid of it. We just need to balance things in a better way, allowing necessary talk but also providing time for people to be alone and quiet when they need it.

This same manuscript [by Merloo] also speaks of "modulations" of silence, various degrees and kinds and levels of silence. Real silence is not isolation. People who live in silence can and do communicate. Silence can carry many different messages; it can be a powerful form of communication. Deep contemplative silence communicates prayer. There's a great difference between the silence of a hermitage and the silence of a community at prayer. From the latter, you get the support of people who love (provided they are awake, of course! Otherwise, the sleep or inertia communicates itself in a dead silence). Therefore, the need is for a true silence which is alive and which carries a loving presence. So genuine silence is not automatic. Neither is noise. The tyranny of noise always has a will behind it. When there's a racket, some person is usually causing it, not the birds or the wind. I visited New York once since entering the monastery, and [in 1964] I went back up around Columbia University and into Harlem. The volume of noise was incredible. It included all-night shootings; two classes of black Muslims were having a kind of war, shooting each other from the roofs. But that was minor compared to the buses on Lenox Avenue, which made an incredible roar. It was like having a jet plane go through your room.

We have to realize that sometimes human beings deliberately create noise. People with frustrated wills come together to make noise that causes others to suffer while they themselves do not suffer. This is one way for a frustrated person to "get even." We have to resist this. There is a note of supreme injustice in noisemaking: the noise made by one person can compel another person to listen. This applies to chitchat as well as to industrial noises.

Since noise is increasing in all directions, the psychology of silence has taken on a special meaning. We are already so adapted to an abundance of screeching sounds that we are surprised when stillness suddenly envelops us. Not that this happens very often! We begin to see that the whole question of our relation to the world, both positive and negative, centers in something like silence. So our service to the world might simply be to keep a place where there is no noise, where people can be silent together. This is an immense service if only because it enables people to believe such a thing is still possible. Think of the despair of people who have given up all hope of ever having a real silence where they can simply be alone quietly. To come to a place where silence exists, to realize there are people who are content to listen and to live in silence impresses people today who are not at all impressed by mere words.

It isn't that words or preaching is bad. It's just that people don't want to hear any more words. In our mechanical age, all words have become alike, they've all been reduced to the level of the commercial. To say "God is love" is like saying "Eat Wheaties." Things come through on the same wavelength. There's no difference, except perhaps in the attitude that is adopted: people know they are expected to look pious when God is mentioned, but not when cereal is! Silence, on the other hand, really does speak to people.

Another aspect of silence is its relation to buildings. No builder today seems to be concerned with the problem of preserving the quiet of the household. The walls of buildings are getting thinner all the time. Ceilings and certain types of new appliances often conduct sounds and noises much better than in the past. Some of our modern buildings are acoustical disasters. Noise pollution has become a major problem in the technological age. Each neighbor knows what the other neighbor does, and neighbors think through a multiplicity of auditory leaks. A friend told me she found herself saying "Bless you" to a sneeze coming through the wall of the next apartment.

The other side of this, of course, is that it's considered a luxury not to be subject to that kind of thing. But should it be a luxury? Buildings could easily be more soundproof. But it's cheaper for them not to be, there's a bigger profit in paper-thin walls. We have to protest this by exercising our right to maintain silence. Our silence is a protest against making people live in buildings that are thrown together with only profit in mind.

Each of these aspects of noise and silence is worth considering. Genuine silence is the fruit of maturity, a blending of many positive and negative aspects. While silence is a form of presence, we must also recognize that presence has to include the notion of distance, the concepts of dignity and reserve. Presence doesn't happen just by people being merged and thrown together. You have to have enough distance to be yourself, composed and at ease. A concentration camp, by contrast, is exactly the opposite of this: officials there try to destroy all distinction between persons, to reduce people to a common lot, to depersonalize as much as possible. This they do by pressing people to the limit, depriving them of food and sleep, and allowing no time for thought or rest until they completely submit. This is what it means to have no distance, no dignity or space in which to be one's own person.

In the contemplative life, too, people must have some distance and time in order to collect themselves. Silence serves this purpose. In the process of becoming an individual, a final separation of personal entities takes place, allowing the mature person to give up infantile magical ties with others and with reality. What are these magical ties? The infant lives in a symbiotic relationship with its mother; while the child is being gestated, the two form but one organism. A magical tie is a kind of symbiotic relationship. It means people get too emotionally involved with each other and then the relationship is no longer really personal. We have all seen situations where people get too wound up in each other, like two parts of one organism. They constantly respond to each other. It's not particularly bad, but it's immature and childish and prevents personhood. It's a sort of magical relationship in which one person surrenders to another, losing distance, and even identity to some extent.

We need to keep a certain distance in order to preserve our identity. A real person has some reserve, some limit, which is good. Reserve or privacy may be described as a subtle psychic vacuum around a person. It is not mere shyness or retreat, nor is it defiance, withdrawal, or introversion. Words like dignity, privacy, reserve, self-respect, distinction, integrity, and diffidence signify the mature state of a psychic entity that can no longer be easily swayed. Even more, they mean that people recognize the necessity and value of a certain distance between human beings, and that they accept this distance in a spirit of stable self-confidence.

Our religious institutes exist to help form human beings, people who are complete persons. This is our work and our duty, to the human race as well as to God. Our monasteries should be producing people who are fully developed human beings and even saints. A saint is more than a fully developed human being. Actually, there's no such thing as a perfectly finished human product in this life. That is often a problem to people who come to see us: they expect a finished product. This is not our fault, it is not the fault of religious orders, nor the fault of our rules. It is the fault of our culture, our background, our history, and our sin.

I once met a Muslim who was an authentic Algerian Sufi. Sufis are Muslims who emphasize the mystical side of religion. This man is a true spiritual master, a very simple person who knows no English and lives in a little back street in Morocco. He has disciples and helps them to advance in the spiritual life. I have seldom met anyone who I thought was closer to being a finished product than this man. He is about eighty-five years old. When he was here a year ago. a lot of us went for a walk with him. When we got to the steep hills, he ran up ahead of everybody. He just kicked his slippers off, picked them up in his hand, and went right up the side of the hill.

This Sufi was invited by Temple University to talk to the students of comparative religion in this country. He visited a lot of centers, not giving formal talks but just enjoying getting together with interested people. He met with a group of about fifteen monks here, and it was amazing how well he understood them. They would ask questions and he would give answers that went far beyond the questions; he would answer what the person really wanted to know. His response was fitted to the person, not in general. That is how true spiritual masters teach.

Do you think people coming to the monastery today can reach the degree of spiritual maturity you've talked about?

Definitely. That's the point of our getting together here, to think about how this can happen. But it's very hard in our culture. Still, with the grace of God there is plenty of hope. We probably won't be able to do this work in a simple way, as some of these people from the Eastern cultures do. They follow a traditional formula and just work hard at it. But for us, there is a whole new thing we have to take note of. We have to keep our traditional values but see them in a new context, in the light of people's experience today. What those now coming to us want is basically the same as what everybody has always wanted: God. Sometimes God is made out to be a great problem. We are told that people have no concept of what God is. But God is not a concept. A person may have no idea of God at all and be completely struck between the eyes by grace. What matters is being spontaneously open to the reality of God.

Would you please say more about the reserve you mentioned?

The study of silence and the idea of dignity and reserve have acquired a new meaning in an age when psychology can become coercive in its policies. Even technology can pry into private lives. We are living in an electronic world where it is possible that a person may have no privacy at all. I am against reducing silence to muteness, against depriving individuals of their right to a many-voiced silence, their right to hear both on the level of grace and on the level of nature. When there's real silence, we're able to hear. And we all need to hear.

God wants to know the divine goodness in us. This is a deep truth, this desire on the part of God to become self-aware in our own awareness. That's why contemplation is for everyone. The purpose of contemplation is not just that we may become aware of God or truths about God, but that God may see the Trinity reflected in each of us, in our own particular identity. It's not necessary to talk to God in order to develop this awareness, although we do this sometimes, for example, in the liturgy, and that's fine. But it's not essential. Are we going to say "I love you"? The more we talk, the more foolish it sounds.

This is where silence comes in. We listen to the depth of our own being, and out of this listening comes a rich silence, the silence of God, which just says "God" or "I am." Now, this is something!

I don't understand why, in all the discussion about God now going on, people are putting aside this fundamental aspect of our life. The claim is made that modern people cannot have an experience of being, that being is not relevant to them. I don't see that. It seems to me that one of the most basic experiences of anyone who gets down into any kind of depth is the breakthrough realization that I am. This is quite normal for any youngster of eight or nine. There's a point in your life where maybe you're just playing around and all of a sudden it hits you between the eyes that you really are. This is a true grasp of what being is. It isn't that you understand a definition of being. You are simply overwhelmed by the fact of being. This is the place where God's reality is going to break through. I become aware of my own reality, and then God's reality turns out to be the ground of mine. The door is there. And now they're telling us this is impossible. Do you have difficulty with this?

It seems to me this breakthrough happens in prayer. I remember, as a child, standing on a hill with everything spread out before me, and suddenly something inside just seemed to burst and I knew there was a union someplace.

Exactly. Wordsworth wrote poems about it. This feeling or intuition comes up everywhere in literature. It's so basic, it is one of the fundamental things God has given us. Perhaps the reason a lot of people don't feel it is that they just don't have time. They never seem able to stop long enough to allow anything to break through. It certainly is not something inaccessible to the human race.

It doesn't stop there, either. After "I am" there is "I am loved."

Yes, and love is not just a sentiment. Love is being itself. It's like a spring coming up out of the ground of our own depths. "I am gift." All that I am is something that's given, and given freely. Being doesn't cost anything. There's no price tag, no strings attached. It's simply given.

That's when we know we're dependent on God and that God is our life.

Exactly. Then we can respond with a complete yes. But this basic sense of our own being can be blocked, maybe by a refusal to take things in terms of gift, or by our not wanting to have to say thanks to anybody. Or maybe we want to have life on our own terms, as if it were not a gift but my due. This attitude goes back to a legalism which is terrible, precisely because, instead of making it possible to accept life as a gift, welling up from within, I make it something that's coming to me, something I'm owed. "I've fulfilled everything. Where's the pay? Where's my merit?"

There's a classic Zen story about this. An old master went from India to China to see the emperor, who was already a Buddhist. The emperor said to the Zen master: "I have built temples, put up pagodas, and started monasteries. What is my reward?" And the master replied: "You don't get any. There's no reward for you." The emperor was all shook up, thought about it, and after a while realized what was meant: If you need something else as a reward, your giving is a fiction.

John Wu, a wonderful fellow, a convert, and a former Catholic ambassador to the Vatican, has written a lot of books and has taught at Seton Hall College for a long time. After translating the Gospel of Saint John into Chinese, he became acquainted with the writings of Saint Teresa of Avila. To his amazement he discovered that she had a lot of ideas very much like those of the old Chinese Taoist philosophers. Dr. Wu really understands this idea of no merit. He went to see Pius XII and got into a disagreement with him because Pius XII said, "Oh, Dr. Wu, you with your wife and your beautiful children! All these are the reward of your virtues." And Wu said, "No, no. No reward!" "Yes, it's the reward." "No, no reward!" Dr. Wu has a very good book on the interior life called *The Interior Carmel,* which is just full of this kind of insight.

There's another Zen story about a fellow who wanted to be a hermit. A rich lady gave him a hermitage at the end of her property. After he had been there about ten years, his benefactor wanted to see if he had made any progress, so she sent down a woman of easy morals to visit him. The woman went to the hermitage, the fellow looked at her blankly, and she went away. When the benefactor went to see him, she said, "I understand someone came to see you. What happened?" He answered, "Nothing." "Did you feel anything?" "I felt like a stone." "Well, you can get out of here," she said, "you're a fake." "What do you mean? I'm a virtuous man." But she said, "Didn't you feel any compassion?" The man was caught on the old ascetic ideal of "You can't faze me, I feel nothing." Just the old ego.

How can we foster this compassion in our lives, feel more for people who are suffering? Do you think we need the daily news in order to be more aware?

We do need to have some access to information about our world, some good magazines and papers. Of course, if you watch TV and read papers constantly, you lose perspective, things get muddied. Anyone who is in the business will tell you that. Political commentators know that if you get immersed in too much news analysis you no longer see anything clearly. It's essential to our life that we have and keep a special perspective. So there's a need to have selected sources available in our communities. No one should *have* to read them.

But anybody who wants to should have access to them. Another reason why we need to have some of these things available is that if you're *not* able to get the news, you can get an exaggerated feeling about how terribly important it is to find out what's going on. When I came to Gethsemani it was just the opposite. The country went to war and the community didn't know it for a week. Pearl Harbor happened on a Sunday and current news items were announced early on Sunday, so it was not until a whole week later that we heard about it. Now, if we had non-commercial TV, I could see its being available all the time. There's nothing intrinsically wrong with TV, it's just a matter of how it's used.

Marshall McLuhan is a person you need to know about. His thought is not always easy to follow, but he's saying that the era of print has come to an end. Before the printing press, we lived in an oral culture in which everything was the spoken word. The invention of print had a great effect on people. It tended to isolate them, whereas the living word implies speakers and hearers. With a book, you can just open it and disappear behind the pages. In classical monastic times, reading did not isolate, because it was done aloud. It was a long time before people just sat and read silently. Saint Ambrose was an exception; he was remarkable for reading silently.

McLuhan points out that now we have masses and masses of printed paper coming out, so much so that people have given up reading. Twenty-eight thousand books are published every year in this country, not counting magazines, papers, catalogues, manuals, and other things. This has a great negative effect on people. The mentality of someone nourished on printed words is different from the person who learns in a predominantly oral culture. TV helps to develop this oral culture, it influences the way people think. Young people who have grown up on TV are apt to be much more intuitive about things that a reading person may not even be aware of, because TV has so much immediacy. Of course, there's a lot of junk on TV, too. McLuhan doesn't seem to take that into account.

I think this explains why young people coming into our life can have such a hard time, because it's so diametrically opposed to this kind of impressionistic culture.

In one way, though, we're closer to them, because books aren't essential to us either. Monastic life is largely oral, even though from the beginning there was some insistence on learning how to read. We've always primarily had a culture of the living word, rather than of writing. The way to live our life is transmitted to us mostly by direct speech. The fact is, of course, that both oral and written communication are necessary. Tapes are part of this, too. Commercial movies can be pretty awful, but there are movies—some may be a bit offbeat or underground—that are worthwhile. Even with a small portable camera some artistic and interesting things can be done. With all of this, it's just a question of balance. Seminars can also be a great help to people like us, something like what we're doing here, no heavy planned agendas, no workshops, but just meeting and gathering together to share experiences. All kinds of possibilities open up in this way.

Before we fold up these sessions we really ought to do a little dreaming out loud. Maybe we could set up some kind of center, nothing official about it, where people like us could come and meet. Maybe invite interesting persons and pick up leads on all sorts of new things. We'd have to be very careful not to turn it into just another summer school or just another workshop. This is a *non-workshop,* we should be anti-workshop. None of this lecture business. Just keep it on an informal basis, nothing prepared, just let things surface. It would be a place where contemplative religious could meet with people in different fields for some account of firsthand experiences, also a place where we could do some purifying of the air. If we could be in dialogue with people looking for meaningful spiritual experience, that could be a good thing, too.

Changing Forms of Contemplative Commitment

Let us suppose that the whole world goes Communist, and the government agrees that this is somehow the answer to all our problems, and contemplative life is over, finished. It's outlawed. Our monasteries are closed down. What then—what do we do?

One of our places in China faced this kind of thing. The monks were dispersed, but about twelve of them remained together and got a simple business going, a little dairy farm. Monastic reform like that is going on in many places. A small group will live together somewhere, in a city or rural area, take jobs, care for one another, pray. The interest in this kind of simple living lies in the fact that it shows us we really don't need a lot of the things we think we do or worry about in order to function as a contemplative group. This new simple way might even be easier than the way we do it. Of course, under the circumstances we described, a contemplative group like that would not be "legal." But neither would the group have to announce itself, there wouldn't have to be any sign that it was a community.

There's a story about three Little Sisters of Jesus, who were living in Japan in a tiny house. They always keep the Blessed Sacrament wherever they are, so a little tabernacle light was burning in their apartment. Some of the Japanese people, none of them Christian, came by and said, "This is a fire hazard." The nuns explained that this light was part of their life of prayer. Immediately there was a change in the visitors. "Fine, fine," they said. Later, the sisters had to go out to work so they no longer burned the light. The Japanese wondered, "What's the matter? They should be praying." In the end they told the sisters, "One of us will take over your job so you can stay here and pray."

You seem to be talking about doing away with the institution.

Not doing away with it, but looking at it carefully.

No one can say to any of us, "You can't be a contemplative anymore." You're a contemplative. I'm a contemplative. That's not something anyone can turn off.

No, you're right. This is the answer. We all know why we're here. The reason is not to our credit. It is God's gift. The gift of God given us in our vocation is something very real and very serious, the most real and serious thing that has ever happened to any of us. We know this. Still, people these days often say, "No, contemplative life isn't real, it isn't important." But there is no need for us to be defensive; we just know better. Renewal for us is getting down to the basic truth of our vocation, which is our liberty as children of God. We have been called to seek God in freedom and to respond to God freely. Who can stop us? We are not crazy, there is no problem. We simply need to share this understanding and stick to it.

So you see that our life can take many forms?

Of course. There are all sorts of possibilities. We have been trained to think only one way and we have emphasized differences between orders. Better not to do this. We all have great traditions and that is fine. But we could all be in the same group if we wished. I mean, just be Christians! I believe we are coming to this more pluralistic view. Renewal is not becoming much more Carmelite or much more Cistercian or much more Franciscan. It's seeing how much each one is already included in the others. I remember one of the big moments early on in my life, when I was trying to decide if I should stay here. It was Good Friday, a really heavy, pressured day back then, and I was exhausted. I was going for a walk in the back of one of the buildings, saying I couldn't stand this place. "I'm a Franciscan, I need nature!" It's funny: the place where I was saying that to myself is precisely where I now cross every day going from the hermitage to the monastery. God was telling me something. I have more nature here than I would have had anywhere. If I'd become a Franciscan, I'd probably be in Paterson!

A question has come up among those in our community who are in the thirty-forty age bracket about the validity of perpetual commitment to a way of life like ours. They ask if that isn't tying down the Holy Spirit. What do you think?

That's a real problem. I think, officially, the Church has already in practice recognized that the trend is certainly away from things like solemn vows. They're almost inconceivable for people today. And the trend is farther away from public vows and more toward something like secular institutes. I think one of the best things that could happen would be to put off the vows so that profession becomes something like the Great Habit in the Oriental rite—that is, something you take after you've been in about twenty years and are *really* committed. The Great Habit is taken after many years of doing more or less active work. Then the monk finally makes a formal commitment to a really contemplative life. He is vowed. He has to be either a hermit or he's got to be at choir more than anybody else and more faithful to everything than others are.

Earlier we talked about wanting to do something but being prevented by the way things are set up. Some people, perhaps rightly, will probably leave and start over somewhere else. This is not as easy as it may look. We have all had experiences with persons for whom something looks good and who want to pursue it, but who end up taking off in a few weeks. There may be some, however, for whom that new way can be a real option.

Most of us, I think, are committed to the institution. For all sorts of reasons, I am absolutely committed to

Gethsemani. So I'm not going to get involved in any new departures. Even though we're quite limited here, we can, without any difficulty, get permission for a day off—anybody. We can take a lunch and go out in the woods for a day, or even get permission to spend several days in a hermitage. These are really fine opportunities.

I'm more and more convinced that our great problem is taking advantage of what we've got. The trouble is, many people seem plagued with problems about the *ideal* situation or problems of conscience. They have a hard time being satisfied with something that is not strictly airtight on all sides. "I've got permission to be in the woods today, but what about next week?" Or, "Is this really the best way for me to search out what I want?" or, "What will be the result of this?" We need to encourage one another to pursue what's available. For example, there's no canonical reason why your groups could not have separate cottages inside the enclosure. All you have to do is do it. One of you talked about a small group of sisters starting something in New England. That's good. But why do people have to sit down and write a rule before they've even had a chance to live awhile? Just take advantage of what is possible within the present situation. For me, that means I can't spend my time worrying about whether my setup is the most perfect one, or whether I have it too good, or whether I'm getting more than I'm entitled to. If my solitude looks like a luxury, I'm still going to hold on to it. Some people may have to start from scratch, but most of us just aren't in shape to do that and don't need to. It's good to have behind us Saints Teresa and John of the Cross, Saints Francis and Dominic and all these great traditions. A lot has been done for us and given to us. Some people feel bad about accepting something like that, but why should we?

If someone wants to be a hermit, that has to come from the community, too. It worked out that way for me and I'm very happy about it. For a long time people here knew I wanted to be a hermit but they didn't put much faith in it. Then one day Dom James said, "Okay, fine." It was voted on by the abbot's Council, and they were unanimous on it. So I really felt the community was behind me. Even if some thought, What is that guy doing up there? it was all right: the community was willing to let me try, and that was understood and accepted on all sides.

I think the hermit, in justice, owes it to the community to be self-supporting. The three of us here more or less do that. One works in the dairy laboratory, testing and doing all the chemical lab work on the milk and cheese. He's a scientist, a former Precious Blood father, who does a very good job. The second one takes a lot of mailing material to his place and works on that. And I have plenty to do. So we're all supporting ourselves. Trouble arises with a hermit who thinks his job is to come back and judge everything that's going on in the community. The only honest thing for us to do is to decide to live simply with what we have. God has given us this and maybe we don't deserve it, but certain things follow from our vocation and we accept them.

What about your work for peace and non-violence?

Without getting into my own work in the peace movement, I do believe we are not entitled to benefit by something like the Vietnam War. And I do work for the political repeal of the draft law because I think the draft is absolutely wrong right now.

When it comes to being non-violent, you have to be very tactful. If you use non-violence simply to tell others that you think they're bad people, this is not a right use. Gandhi did not do it that way. When Gandhi did a non-violent action, it was crystal-clear why he did it. For instance, the poor people of India had to pay tax on their salt, which was obviously unjust. So Gandhi gathered the people together and they walked six or seven hundred miles to the sea. On the seashore they made salt. They took seawater and dried it out. They did a symbolic gesture of making free salt and then walking back. They didn't get much salt, but something was made quite clear. They were saying, "You have no right to stop us from getting salt from water." Salt was obviously a human necessity and everybody saw this. The English saw it. Non-violent actions have to be clear, not mysterious. The point of non-violence is to make other persons see that something is as true for them as for you. Others have to be able to see and agree, from what you are doing, that there is a higher truth which is better than what they're committed to. That is difficult. Martin Luther King, Jr., did it with the Montgomery bus strike. It was made quite clear. The meaning of the non-violent action has to be understood each time.

There is one very good non-violent group you might keep praying for, called the Committee of Southern Churchmen. Most of the members are Protestant. One of their leaders is a friend of mine, Will Campbell, a marvelous fellow who visits here often. He preaches to the Ku Klux Klan and is a friend of the head of the Klan in North Carolina, Raymond Cranford. When Cranford's wife was sick, Will fetched bedpans for her and took care of her. All the while he kept saying to the Cranfords, "You've got to be reconciled." Will understands that much more is involved than simply convincing others. He tries to maintain a line of communication, breaking down not only the prejudice on one side but also the barrier on the opposite side that says "KKK: inhuman." This is a Christian view of things.

This is what we have to do: avoid lining up on the side of a revolution as well as on the side of a counter-revolution. We need to line up on the side of the people. Wherever there is human presence, we have to be present to it. And wherever there is a person, there has to be personal communication. There Christ can work. Where there is presence, there is God. A Christian is one who continues to communicate across all the boundaries, a sign of hope for a convergence back to a kind of unity.

But meanwhile, it seems that the white race will recognize the black race only when it is understood that economically or politically the blacks are advantageous to the whites.

That's American pragmatism. And certainly change will not come out of pure benevolence. We have to look at this problem with stark realism. Even if some families in those gracious old Southern mansions treated blacks well, that image is a dead myth. Racism is real. In Harlem, one sees thousands and thousands of blacks that no white person even knows exist. A further tragedy about the slums is that a poor black family in the tenements pays more proportionately for what it is not getting than a family on Park Avenue pays.

This is true in the neighborhood stores in Mississippi, too. The people can't get to the shopping centers, so they have to pay more for milk and bread and everything else. They make far less and have to pay more.

This is a terrible thing. But the people have caught on now, they know what is happening to them. Put yourself in the position of a woman who for many years paid on insurance for her father, only to have some little clause cheat her out of it when he died. There's no moral theology that says such people are stealing when they take advantage of riots to claim what is theirs. I read a heartbreaking story about a poor old woman in Newark who was picked up during the riots and arrested for stealing some canned goods. The police took her to the station and called her "Miss American Shoplifter" of the year. A cruel thing. We cannot live life without thinking about these things. If we put ourselves in a different world, we are not being true.

There aren't answers to these problems. It will take an enormous amount of planning from the top. But we have to do what we can, we have to hope and pray that the greed of people who profit by all this will not hold. The reason things aren't changed is that somebody is making money from the present situation. We have to learn to dissociate ourselves from those who are profiting. The problem comes because they may be our benefactors. How do we know? Saints in the Middle Ages refused to take money from a bishop who got it from simony. What are we going to do? It is a moral problem, and we can't be pharisaical about it.

It is amazing to me that Christianity is the most wonderful thing that has ever come to us and yet it seems to have touched the lives of most people very little.

Isn't that the way it is all through the Bible? It seems to me that that is part of the message. Maybe that's the meaning of "Many are called, but few are chosen." It isn't that people are consciously bad. Maybe they respond on one level but just do not follow through. Scripture teaches us basic things, God's thoughts about human beings. We have to remember that no one does everything right. We are all sinners. God speaks and we do not listen. On the other hand, the mercy of God is constant. It cannot be overcome. God's promises are absolute. Being Christian doesn't mean "being on the right side." A Christian does not always know where justice lies, does not always see clearly. But the Christian is aware that, while in the human being there is falsity and infidelity, in the mercy of God there is always absolute fidelity. So we reject no one, but still try to dissociate ourselves from anything that is going to hurt other people. Every Christian has to stand up for the truth that God's mercy is without repentance. God never takes back mercy. We are in a world where many people are in despair. That's where God is really needed. Our Christian witness of mercy is not, after all, credible to a lot of people, because it's not very profound. That is why we have to bear witness to the word of God. The renewal of the whole Church hinges on this. And not just in ideological terms. We also have to dig in and really help those in trouble.

Let's try to sum up here what we've been talking about so far. First of all, I do get the impression that something worthwhile is happening with us, that we are creating a kind of community among ourselves. Secondly, there seems to be no doubt that we all have confidence in our vocation, that we know what we are doing and why we are doing it, and that our life is worth our best efforts. It follows from this that it is good for us to get together like this, so that we can experience our unity and confirm one another in some substantial way.

Another thing which comes through is that we are all very much committed to the communities we're in, that we have no particular need to start something fantastically new. Others can do this. We admire them, but we ourselves are able to live in our present community structure, even though it is not ideal and there are a lot of things wrong with it. And we're not worried about making our institutions "relevant." If they are more or less working in such a way that we are able to accomplish what we are called to accomplish, then it doesn't matter what others think about them. Certainly our setup has to be meaningful to the people coming in, or it isn't going to last very long. But there is a difference in that kind of relevance; it's not the relevance of the institution but the relevance of the community. These are two very different things, institution and community. For most of us, the institution is much less relevant than the community. We have a very good community here and I'm not worried about the institution anymore. Superiors may have to worry a little, but what matters is the community as a place where God is present and a place where the Spirit is working.

One of the practical things we need to talk about is how to maintain a really effective and useful communication among ourselves and other contemplative communities who are interested in the same things. Valuable new ideas and vital information need to keep circulating, whether everyone understands this or not. This is definitely something the Church needs. We should be able to help one another judge what is useful and good and to prop one another up, as it were, by looking at things together. When contemplative communities are just left on their own, things can easily get distorted or pushed aside. You can get a false picture if isolated on a little island.

Responsibility in a Community of Love

Yesterday we started off on our very unofficial way. I was surprised at how much came out of it. Several valuable points came up: silence and noise, presence, a little about relationships, something on the race question and non-violence, some other basics of our vocation. We all seem very clear about our own commitment and how worthwhile it is. So today we'll go on with things like that.

One of the basic questions is how not to make our institutions look dynamic or "with it." We have no obligation to look good on somebody else's terms. If we try doing that, we'll be out of date in three years. That's about how long these new groups last. We do have a real obligation to respond to the Word of God. Even more, there's an obligation to a prophetic call, given to us poor people, just as we are, none of us practicing heroic poverty or anything like that. We're not living in slums. But even in our somewhat rigid institutions, I think we can be prophetic.

After our discussion yesterday I was thinking about how so much of our training taught us to "go ask the priest." We were not to make a decision or judgment on our own. We just didn't think in those terms.

Now's the time. There are plenty of sisters smart enough to do that, who certainly have better judgment about their own situations than someone outside. Priests you consult may often have no concept of what your life is about, what your order means, what your needs are. All they can do is look in a book and dig up a canon, and they may not know too much about that, either.

*What about nuns who are so fearful and inhibited that they
cannot make independent judgments? They can really hold
a community back.*

I think they have to be encouraged to go ahead and make
judgments. They need to be put in situations where they
have to. The old system, of course, did not provide for this.
It was fixed so that an individual never had to make judgments but would just sit in line waiting to ask the Superior,
"May I have a toothbrush?" This is absurd. We built things
this way and called it the Cross or obedience. This may have
been all right if you were living in Austria in 1772 under an
absolute emperor, and all you had to do was to keep the institution going, because it had been endowed. But we're not
doing that anymore.

*What about some kind of publication to get ideas like this
circulated?*

It wouldn't be hard to get something started on a mimeograph
basis, maybe publish some things later. Contemplatives in
America need some kind of intercommunity forum of opinion. But don't get involved in printing. I could help a little, but
sisters should do this themselves. Just something unofficial in
which you can express yourselves. Like being here together—
it's completely informal. You came for retreat and we are able
to talk together.

*Whenever we ask permission, it seems the issue gets all
bungled up.*

Exactly, so don't ask. I mean, unless you absolutely have to.
The whole bent of the Church at this moment is for change.
And therefore change has the benefit of the doubt.
Obviously, the spirit of the Council is that we're supposed
to experiment, take risks, change, and develop. This has the
stamp of the Holy Spirit on it. Just as obviously, there are
people on top who are scared, who want to stop it. They
take second place right now. A prudential Christian decision
now is in favor of courageously following what the Council

clearly wants, and the Council clearly wants development. People who do not want development have to prove their point very hard before one can follow them in conscience. If everybody obeyed all the curial officials in everything in every moment, there would be no progress possible. There would be no point in having had a Council, no point in John XXIII having been Pope.

At the same time, there has to be caution and respect. We don't act rebelliously or out of contempt, but just quietly go along with what the Council wants. Experiment is the order of the day, so make experiments. Just be careful not to do crazy things. Trouble comes when people want to make an issue of everything, when they want not just to change but also to win. Wanting to chalk up a score is bad. This is not a game of besting the Curia or the authorities. We have to be clear on that. We're not trying to get points for our side. We just want to do what God wants. If we can once get this distinction clear, that's all the authorities care about. Much of this other side business is face-saving. If people are obviously needling and insulting authorities, of course the latter will try to save face. But if you're considerate and in good faith, you won't be bothered much. People in authority have sense enough to see the difference. I go my way quietly, saying all kinds of things that are very unpopular and that many people don't like at all. But they're not going to fool with me, because I'm not fighting them. I'm simply saying what I think I ought to say. I am not challenging anyone.

Would you say something about each person in a community contributing to its support?

That is definitely a part of community life. Obviously, the hermits here contribute their support, as they should. It seems to me that ways of doing that can always be found. Don't you think so? Certain kinds of work can be done in a hermitage just as well as anywhere else. There has to be real responsibility. A hermit has to be, first of all, on the level, contributing something to his support. The community, in turn, provides food and other necessities. In monastic life, this should be an aspect of community. My place in this community is up in the woods, but it is my place in the community.

Do you think a cloistered community should be self-supporting?

I think it certainly should be, if possible. We should try. But not every cloistered community can be self-supporting. It's a hard question, but it's becoming a necessity. In Europe it has been a necessity for a long time. In our country we are still in a privileged position, but it isn't going to be that way much longer.

The mail is full of appeals from religious organizations, lots of them.

Soon it will be really difficult to get by. Even here. We would have a hard time if a depression hit, because we produce cheese and fruitcake, which are for a luxury trade.

Do you think there is anything to continuing the idea that a contemplative monastery should be a center of art and culture? And that talented sisters should be encouraged to develop their creative gift? This is tied up with the question of being self-supporting.

I think if they have real talent, and can integrate it into the life, they should be encouraged. We have a very good artist here and his art is helping his life. But the answer to your question really depends on the community and on each case. At the same time, in every community, one has to accept doing some boring things. I should talk! I've always had a lot of work that I like and am interested in. But we've all had to do routine and boring work, things that aren't creative.

Art is a very real kind of work. There are some fantastic artists in Europe in some of the monasteries and some excellent poets. These people are solid and there's no problem with them. As for newcomers, I think they have to be tested a bit. It's tricky, because art can be an escape; people can just enter into a little world of making ceramics. Real art is a vocation and not an avocation; one has to mean business. Still, one doesn't make money on art.

What is your opinion concerning requests for home visits? Do you see this as in keeping with our dedication to contemplative life?

My feeling is that it should not be absolutely excluded, that it should not be impossible. We have to take into account a new view of this question. I would say there should be a chance to go home. The community itself should decide. With us and our spirit, it's entirely in the hands of the abbot. This is the old way of looking at it. In modern thought, it's for the community to make up its mind on this. If the community feels more or less unanimously that sisters ought to be able to go home, then one could take that as a sign of God's will.

Of course, there are a number of angles to this question. For instance, we say "Honor thy father and mother," yet fathers and mothers are somewhat less honored at the present time than they were in the past. In the past, when families were close, it was still possible for a family to accept a real cutoff when it came to religious life. Today people are often ambiguous about whether they really do love Father or Mother. They need to prove it more to themselves. I think this is unconscious in the younger generation. There's a great deal of insecurity, psychologically, about their love for parents, something which in former days people never questioned much.

Neither of our postulants wants to go out, but in both cases their parents do not understand.

I've had novices and young monks who feel that way. They do it unconsciously as a kind of punishment for their parents. They're getting back at them for something. Usually, it's a rigid fellow with a certain stereotyped kind of mind. Sometimes, in direction, I'll say, "Well, what do you hear from home?" And he says, "I'm not writing to my mother." And I say, "Listen, man, what do you mean?" I had a big fight with one novice about that. He said, "I'm dead to my mother." Behind this was a sticky situation, a broken family, and this young man blamed his mother for his feeling like an orphan. Sometimes those who are most strict about not wanting to see their parents may be carrying a little grudge, or a desire to punish. But, of course, this may not be the case here at all.

What do you think about sisters from active orders spending time in the monastery?

There's more than one way to look at that, too. I think we would all agree that it's necessary for people to have something like that available to them, and not just an ordinary retreat house. Many in active orders are now founding little houses of prayer for their congregations. They need to find out how contemplative orders actually live and work. The only way they can do that is to participate in the life of a community. You would be doing a real act of charity to let them come in and get some experience. I would say that almost all of us could certainly do that much sharing with someone who seriously wants to find out about contemplative life.

When these people come, let them join in the work, take part in all the regular things. They probably would need to stay for several months in order to get a real feel for the life, because time is different for us. I think it would be necessary to go through at least part of the liturgical cycle and a number of feasts in order to get a true sense of the life. By participating as fully as possible, these people will learn a great deal. Each community has to determine for itself what is appropriate and good.

Could you elaborate more on our end as contemplative communities? You mentioned something about being charismatic or prophetic.

Charismatic is a word that can mean a lot of different things. It's hard to define. I would say something charismatic is a gift from God to follow a special kind of freedom. That's why it's essential for the contemplative life not to be tied up in routine activity, for instance, parish work, where one has to be at a certain place at a certain time on a regular basis. We are free from that in order to have a much more flexible and much more unexpected kind of development. This is not to say that a lot more is happening, but it does mean we should not be held by anything other than the inspiration of the Holy Spirit. What does "inspiration of the Holy Spirit" mean in our life?

To begin with, inspiration is a judgment on a deep level, somewhere down in the ground of our being. It is central and fundamental, not superficial. It is a kind of orientation pointing toward our real goal. An inspiration of the Holy Spirit may have nothing to do with anything terribly important in itself, but it gives us the conviction that when we follow through on this ordinary thing, we are on the right track. We need to be free for that. We are not in our monasteries simply saying prayers. We are remaining open to something, the unexpected. Something is going on at a deep level.

Of course, this happens in other kinds of life. But this is our whole job. Others have this, plus another job, like teaching children, for example, and the Holy Spirit is using them to do that. With us, it's simply that God is calling us to be always available. It's not easy to put a precise finger on this. One element in this aspect of our life is a kind of long emptiness, which should perhaps not be interfered with. It is a desert life as opposed to the fullness and preoccupation of an active life, where satisfaction comes from achieving things. We have a definite area of non-achievement. We have to feel that we are not necessarily accomplishing anything much. This is important for us.

Would you say something about prayer, please?

Certainly, our life is one of prayer. Traditionally, the basic reason for contemplative life was to pray without ceasing. The conferences of John Cassian are a classic source on that. He speaks of purity of heart, which has a special meaning in the tradition. Cassian says that purity of heart is the aim of our life; more specifically, the aim of the ascetic life. All the things we do, like praying, reading, working, fasting, vigils, have only one purpose: to bring us to purity of heart. Cassian describes purity of heart as a state in which you are more or less interiorly free, not bound to any particular project or particular work. You have the ordinary human concerns, but you're not tied to them. Above all, you're not bound by concepts. You're not preoccupied with reasoning about God. Purity of heart is a state of prayer in which you're concerned directly with God, without the medium of concepts or actions or a lot of affections. You're just there. Somehow or other, if you don't try to pin it down too much, there's simply the realization that you're with God in some mysterious way that can't be explained.

True purity of heart means not being concerned with yourself, not even being aware of yourself. Saint Anthony says that perfect prayer begins when we no longer know we are praying, when we do not even know we are there. This is universally valid thinking on the purpose of the ascetic life; we make of it what we can. It is, more or less, a state of total freedom from any concern with oneself.

Every spiritual tradition has something related to this: John of the Cross, Francis, Bonaventure, Thomas, Dominic, Alphonse. Dominican nuns, immersed in Eckhart and the Rhenish mystics, were tremendously important in the Rhineland, where the friars were going around carrying on a fantastic movement of prayer which swept through the whole of that area in the fourteenth and fifteenth centuries. This is our kind of territory, though we rarely advert to it. Prayer is where charism operates. And prayer and charism lead to a pure heart.

This state of purity of heart and emptiness is what we are for, certainly. Apart from actual movements of grace, actual little lights and inspirations, there remains this atmosphere of emptiness and disposability, of being totally at the disposition of God. "I am free. Do with me what you want." And God does, in various ways. The sense that you cannot pinpoint it, cannot do anything to prove it, cannot argue about it, is fine. There's no need to talk about it to anyone, unless you find a friend of like mind who understands. And even then, it's better to allude to it vaguely. You do not have to describe anything.

This ties in with what we were saying earlier about silence and community, and it is very important for the contemplative life. Let's hope that at least a few people among us are deeply into this disposition of prayer and purity of heart. It's what we are all about.

This way of living is prophetic, not in the sense of sudden illuminations as to what is going to happen at some future moment, but in the sense that we are so one with the Holy Spirit that we are already going in the direction the Spirit is going. You can, in some way, anticipate things in the Church and you're ready for what is coming along. Or perhaps not! It doesn't matter that much. But there can be a sense of what is needed. Our life is meant to give us that kind of sensitivity and that kind of atmosphere, a state of real humility and peace and simplicity.

This reminds me of a book on Our Lady, in which her position among the apostles, for instance in the descent of the Holy Spirit, is described as a "dispositive" cause.

This is real Thomist language! There is a French Dominican, Paul Philippe, formerly secretary of the congregation for religious, who has some marvelous writing on Mary and on her life of prayer, for which there was absolutely no pattern. He describes it as a complete "no-man's-land" because everything was new. Mary was absolutely and totally free in an immediate relationship to God for which there was no precedent. It was beyond prophecy. Mary is the Queen of Prophets, far beyond all of them in this purity of heart and virginity of spirit. The early Church writers say that this kind of virginity of spirit is what prepared Mary for the virgin birth. This is all part of our tradition.

Doesn't this come close to saying what is meant about the Church's need for contemplatives?

Exactly. We should be keeping this kind of freedom alive in the Church, freedom in relationship to God. This means something to those who understand it, but there's no need to explain it. People will come to see it if we are not bothered about being understood.

Community will grow if we let it be more natural and spontaneous, because the kingdom of heaven is like yeast. The yeast that comes to us most spontaneously is natural friendship. The grace of God is with us and we just need to let it work. But we're slow to believe this. Of course, sometimes it's quite hard to believe that grace is with us, because there seems to be something in the system that wants to cage up the Holy Spirit.

One of the things about our kind of community is that we have people among us whom we would not necessarily have picked as friends. But the grace of God is working there. The fact that there's a normal inclination to share things with people is a sign of God's will. We've had so much trouble with the old idea that, because we naturally like someone, it is wrong. Not at all. There are likes and likes; one has to distinguish between mature and immature friendships.

If people come to our communities because they have the same ideals and bring this natural spontaneity with them, then what is militating against this continuous growth you speak about?

I think back to when I entered here. There always seem to be two opposite poles. There is, first, the fact of loving the community, of loving the life. There's a kind of drawing to the whole feel of the life. We can even like the setup because of some of the strictness, since this firmness helps create the situation we want. I liked this place because it was strict. But at the same time, I could see that the austerity was sort of inhuman. It bothered me less than it bothers people coming today, probably because I am basically a European and have been through a French boarding school! I would hate to have to go through that now. But it is possible not to mind if things are a bit artificial, some people can laugh them off. But this is no longer true, young people now cannot do that. It's not worth it to them, they do not have the motives. I suppose I felt that I could serve God and be happy doing it, and this other stuff didn't matter that much, even though it was irritating and a little stupid. But now we are beginning to see that this kind of life has harmed people. And we are realizing that just the ability to live through such a regimen is no particular achievement. What made it inhuman was that it was presented as being what mattered.

This was all the result of a certain kind of culture. We can understand it better when we know the history of the Council of Trent and even of the Middle Ages. We are shocked at the Middle Ages, and there was a lot that was wrong. But it was a very alive and spontaneous period, even though strict and tough.

Cistercian life in the Middle Ages had lots of adventure in it. Monks would take monastery wine to a distant town and be attacked by pirates on the way down the Rhine. In northern England, where there were great expanses of moorland with sheep, three brothers might be stuck twenty miles from nowhere. They had to have a real capacity for making decisions on their own. And they did. Saint Bernard was an extremely independent man. He spoke boldly to the Pope and to lots of people. We may think of the Middle Ages as a time of great submission. Not at all. But, at the end, Trent came along, and the Protestants, and we fell into all kinds of defensive positions. Legalism said we were safe and secure if we followed the letter of the law. We can do this, instead of loving. But that is real abuse, and deadness, in our life.

This letter-of-the-law approach stunts growth and it stunts contemplation: you sit for half an hour, you're there, you're a contemplative. This is like doing time, like being in prison. There is no love. We have to do something about that. Deep down is the real thing, that which we would do even if everything else collapsed, what we would do no matter how bad things are. There is one thing we are looking for: God.

The purpose of the community is expressed in both wrong ways and right ways. The wrong way has to do with guaranteeing regularity, because this gives a kind of legal security. This approach ruins community, if community becomes a matter of fidelity to a certain kind of structure, it's over. We have to do all we can to break up this kind of legalistic mentality, even with people who seem unable to change. Those who can't change will do harm if others just wait for them. We can't hold back everything because of these people. But we are brothers and sisters, we have to live together, so some accommodations must be made. Cruelty in the name of community life—no matter who does it, the people needing to change or the people who don't see the need—is simply not compatible with love.

So the question arises: Can we regroup? And how? People who want more activity can group together, and persons who want more contemplation can get together. This regrouping is going on all over the Church. There are the legalistic types and the freer types. Maybe the best thing to do is to regroup into separate houses. If people can come around, there is no problem. If others are impatient and want to move fast, then let them go and do something special.

But aren't we meant to work out things together? We chose to gather as a community and we choose to support one another in aspiring to a common end. We are a protection to one another in doubt. Sometimes I think "contemplative community" is a contradiction.

Oh, I don't think so at all. A community really equals love. And contemplation is not an individualistic matter, it takes place in a cultural context. Community means a place in which it is most simple and easy for anybody who's going to be a contemplative to be one, because of the community. But community is not just a means. It's an end, too. We each have our personal end and our communal end. Unity and diversity. Community is one end. Then people have diversity of function in this community.

Let's look at a Gospel text. Here is John, 14:32: "If you

love me, you will keep my word. And my Father will love you and we will come to you and make our home with you." Now, what is "my word"? Christ's word is: *Love one another.* Community. Live in community, have community of love, let God dwell right here among you. God is experientially present, and we are aware that God is with us. This is contemplation, isn't it, the experience of the nearness and closeness of God? Therefore, if we love, the love which makes us love one another in community is that which makes us contemplatives. Because we love, God is present. Contemplation is presence. The presence of love to one another goes with the presence of God to oneself. It is in community that this Presence realizes itself through our love. Love of God, love of one another. Praising God together, praising God individually. Seeking God together, seeking God individually.

"Those who do not love me, do not keep my word. My word is not my own, it is the word of the One who sent me. I have said these things to you, also with you. But the Advocate, the Holy Spirit, whom the Father will send in my name, will teach you everything and remind you of all that I have said to you." So once again, where there is community, love, obedience, there the Holy Spirit is present. There the Holy Spirit teaches us, reminds us of everything that Jesus said, and makes it live in us. It all goes together. At certain moments we are together as a community and we all help one another to remember the things of God. The Holy Spirit is more present in that way. At other times we are not together, we are alone and praying silently, solitarily. It all works together. There's an alternation.

The thing to do is to create a community in which the source of contemplation is this kind of love. I came to the monastery seeking a deep personal union with God, and I believe my brothers did the same. So we all want the same thing for each other. We tend to do it in various ways, sometimes in liturgy, sometimes with the diversity of our gifts. This applies to any community, in terms of seeking contemplation.

I think my problem with community is the fact that often it means just being together, doing things together, having no friends outside the community. But this community of love together, that I can see as an end in itself.

Certainly, it should not be exclusive, that community members are the only people we love. Our friends should be able to come visit and they can also become friends of others in the community. Sometimes we share our families, too. This is good.

When we talked about community before, we said we wanted freedom but, at the same time, that we can easily put the Holy Spirit in a cage. I think we don't want to lose our life and that we're being very cagey now.

In practical cases, I think young people can too quickly go off to start something new. It looks good but collapses all too soon. This makes us hesitant about experiments. Community is involved because community has been so abused and people really are looking for a community of love. And for real friendship. Maybe they are trying to force it to happen and that won't work, of course. They may feel there is no chance whatever of anything really happening in the accepted kind of community structure. So they need to take the risk. I think we ought to support them rather than turn them off. We have some experimentation in the order, but many have had to leave.

This could be a revitalization of the whole group.

Exactly. For years I have been encouraging our having different kinds of small house experiments, with the big house here as a kind of center and basic support. If an experiment fails, those who wanted could easily return to the original group.

If our communities were more flexible, sisters might not feel they had to move to a faraway place or to the city. At the least, we could make some things more flexible and give people more room.

If sisters need more solitude in community, I would think

they could do a kind of work that is apart from the others. There are lots of people who would be satisfied with just a little more solitude in connection with community. I don't see any problem with giving it to them. There's no harm in just sticking down a hermitage at the end of the garden, or getting a property where there is more room and some woods. If you are not in the country, I would say you should get there. Do all you can to get away from the large population centers where there is a lot of noise. A large community that can support people should. A smaller one can do all it can to support sisters who need more solitude.

I think it's important to know what the Church looks to us for. And I mean the Church, the pulsating, vibrant body of the Church, not the hierarchy. Won't that Church miss us if we don't live in community?

Yes, I think so. The Church needs communities of people who are serious enough about contemplation to get together and live it and to make all kinds of sacrifices to do it, to give up other things to do it. This is a witness. But we don't need to bother being aware of it. Just accept the fact that we belong where we are and we're doing something that the Church needs. We can get into the business of asking what role we are fulfilling. If we're too conscious of a role, it's going to get in the way.

The nature of the Church being what it is, I can't possibly fulfill any role except under the impulse of the Spirit.

Oh yes, you can! But the Church needs people who are determined to follow the call of the Spirit to seek God in some way. It needs us, needs charismatic contemplative communities, prophetic communities, people who are not afraid to speak out when they have to, or to shut up when they have to, or to go out into the woods when they have to. If no one sees them anymore, they just disappear. That's their charism. The Church needs me to live my own life, for good or bad reasons. If the communities we are in are not helping us, we have to do it on our own.

On one level, we can do some things within our present structures. But this probably falls short of what is required of contemplative life as a whole, although it's probably fine for most of us. I think contemplative life does need these new experiments, new opportunities, and possibilities. This is where the younger generation comes in. If someone is trying something new and it flops, we ought to be there as a kind of safety net for them to land in. This is a work of charity. The fact that some experimental things fail is sad, but it is more sad that—if and when this happens—we are not there for them in some way.

Do you think these experiments fail because there has not been enough preparation?

I don't really know. I don't think the persons themselves know. Perhaps their aims are too ambiguous. With so many opportunities to explore, maybe they can't find a definite direction. A lot of it strikes me as too much improvising. Dom Winandy of Belgium has a good idea going in British Columbia, with about a dozen other people, including some ex-Trappists. They have no community structure whatever, no institution. Occasionally, they have to turn in an account of their expenses. They also have to earn their own living, but I don't know how they do that. It might be by begging: we get a lot of begging letters from former members! They have no meetings, no common liturgies, no common exercises. They are hermits, the Hermits of Saint John the Baptist. Each one builds his own shack, as best he can. This seems to work, because this man [the founder] is very spiritual and well-formed, quite definite about what he's doing, able to give people all kinds of liberty. He is not their Superior, but a spiritual father. They can get as much or as little advice as they need. If a man can mind his own business and live in his hermitage and do what he's doing, he's there for life.

The bishop must trust him very much. That's something our women's communities need: for church authorities to trust us.

That's very important. If you want to set up something official, the bishop or the chapter needs to okay it. But you could certainly try something unofficial. We have to break out of this image thing—this "cloistered mystique." And why doesn't someone do a mimeographed paper of some kind that could circulate around, where you could express your own opinions? It's worth thinking about.

Vocation: "The Time When You Were Called"

We have to ask ourselves: Where do we look for new openings? Where is the light coming from? We are obviously assailed on all sides by a lot more than just what is relevant for us. I'd like to experiment a little with a newspaper article on the "revolution" that is sweeping the convents. We definitely need to cultivate a kind of independent power to criticize things like this that come our way. Of course, we're already doing this to some extent. It's good to be able to read and sort out what makes sense and what doesn't.

You've probably all read this recent article, "A Catholic Nun Undergoes a Revolution." It talks about "new patterns of living for the once-cloistered sisters." Right away you get a monumental impression of ex-Carmelites, ex-Poor Clares, ex-us. After you read awhile you find out they're talking about sisters who, strictly speaking, have never been cloistered at all. So the first thing to discover is that what they're not talking about is cloistered or once-cloistered people. You have to start the story by forgetting their thesis. The topic sentence goes out the window. After you get past this, you find that what the sisters themselves are saying makes sense. But what they say is embedded in a mishmash of all kinds of misleading comments. So that if someone has left the "cloister" to become a dentist, the implication is that this is what contemplatives really ought to do. This is silly, of course. When reading things like that, people don't apply logic. They skim along on the key words and pick up things that move them emotionally. So when they get to the end of the article, Mr. and Mrs. Average Catholic are left with a vague conviction that the Carmelites are all dentists now. It's probably better that way—at least they're doing something useful!

A little farther on, the article describes two sisters who "are spending much of their time producing children's shows for commercial TV." Now, there's nothing wrong with producing shows for TV. But the key word here is *commercial,* telling us they've finally come into the world of reality. *Commercial* equals *real.* This is what's so bad, because for anybody with any kind of sense, who is outside all this, commercial TV spells *unreality,* and spells everything that is phony and a waste of time. This is supposed to be a claim to relevance in the modern world. If we really want to be relevant, we should be getting into *non-commercial* television. Then we can finally get some straight news and decent programs. Actually there are people who are doing very good non-commercial TV. But so much TV is useless.

Another bit of nonsense from this article: "Although it brings religious instruction to the children, the format of *The Little Flock* is kept informal and a classroom style is avoided." Here again, this is real smart, putting something across without your knowing it. Isn't that great? They are slipping in the religious message subliminally, so this brings us right up to date with the modern world. This is another example of a completely mythical and stupid view of our relation to the world. The assumption is that one relates to the world by getting into business, where deceiving everybody else is okay if one does it smartly and smoothly.

We have to be attuned to these things. A true cloistered spirit should include the ability to screen out things like this and not accept them. Living a contemplative, disciplined life should help us see what's artificial. But, unfortunately, we can get caught up just like anyone else. We're in the same danger of thinking, That's it, that's right. The point is, there has to be some discrimination and critical judgment.

Now here's a nun speaking wisely, I think. She says that you can be just as effective in an area nobody seems to think important as you can in the poorest corner of a ghetto. This is pure gold. To feel that you don't have to be in something that's going to get a great press and a lot of publicity, something that no one thinks is important and doesn't appear to be heroic, can be very worthwhile. This brings up the question of poverty, which is dubious for many people and for us, too. Because there is no perfect poverty for any kind of American today. No matter what we do, we're one of the millionaires of the earth. We're living in a society which has got rich off the rest of the world. There's no way around it. Even if we wear a gunny sack, we're still American. We've grown up in this economy. We've been put through college on it. We've profited by it. And our convents have been built by it. The only possibility I can see of getting around it is by becoming another Benedict Joseph Labré in North Africa, where we'd last about ten minutes! As soon as people found out we were Americans, that would be it. So we simply have to practice the kind of poverty we can. Even though it's not that relevant, it can be real in our life and contribute to the development we are meant to achieve.

"As a religious who is a dentist, I hope to exemplify the Christian life at the professional level." Instead, I would say, just be a dentist. For example, I am simply a writer. I no longer write anything specifically religious, except when asked. I write poetry that has no explicit message. On the other hand, there is such a thing as preaching the Word. "But there's a lot that can be done by attitude and approach." Yes and no. Just go ahead and do what you have to do.

Here's another text from a new magazine called *Motive*. It's a book review of a science-fiction novel that has a lot to say about the future of religion. In this imaginative story, set in the year 2000, a human child somehow visits Mars and then comes back to earth with a new religion. This strange religion or church is a kind of parody of modern, popular religion in America. The worship service involves good sales-convention techniques and lively audience participation. Spot advertisements have become a lucrative part of each service. "Products can be even more closely allied to church interests. Send your child to school with a bulging box of Archangel Cookies, each one blessed and wrapped in an appropriate text. And pray that each goodie given away may lead a child of sinners to the light."

Incidentally, did I ever tell you the Chinese fortune cookie story? You know how the printed fortune slip comes out of the cookie. Three people are in a Chinese restaurant eating fortune cookies. The first one opens up a cookie and the paper says: "You will be rich and famous." Another opens one and it says: "You will be happily married within two months." And the third one opens up the cookie and reads: "Help! I'm a prisoner in a Chinese cookie factory."

Back to our parody on religion. There's more to it. What happens is that gradually there develops a kind of religious elite, in contrast to the popular religion. This gets close to us. It's not our contemplative life that's being proposed but the real need on the part of many people for a deep kind of spiritual experience. This is the point. Here is someone projecting that by the year 2000 conventional religion will be more or less gone, except for the commercial business. But there is this elite, looking for a real spiritual discipline. The main character says: "The faith I was reared in didn't require anybody to know anything. And a major part of this new discipline is learning the Martian language. The languages of the earth are inadequate for understanding and expressing the new universalism." One Martian word sums up what it's all about, the word *grock*. *Grocking* is really a form of prophetic intuition which is able to project forward and to anticipate what's coming, so that people in this religious elite, by virtue of their discipline and their study of the Martian language, are *grocking* what's ahead.

This is what we're all supposed to be able to see and do now, to anticipate what's coming. Recently a book came out which applies this idea to Christianity. It says the Christian should be able not only to be orthodox but also to see what's going to happen and to make it happen. This is the Marxist view of things: you get in the know about the laws of history and you are so smart and so disciplined that you can make things move in that direction.

You can imagine the amount of plain old pride in that, and how wrong it can all be—the party decisions made, the party always being right. Stalin got allied with Hitler, which nobody expected; he did just the right thing at the right moment. And Hitler turned around and tried to do him in. But no, he [Stalin] was right: he was just making history ahead of time. *Grocking* is something like that. The reviewer says that it is "a rejection of faith in favor of demonstrable truth and hard discipline." He says many of the new generation are sympathetic to it, because they have observed faith used as an excuse for not asking the hard questions, and disappointed that real discipline wasn't required in their churches. This is now a critique of present-day religion.

"At the heart of the new religion is the affirmation and greeting regularly used with the fellowship: Thou art God." And then: "All that grocks is God." Now we see that to be a member of this elite community is to have the mind of God, to have a kind of prophetic capacity. But note that all this is arrived at by pride, by self-perfecting, by discipline. Pretty soon, you can discard all the non-elite, they can be *spilled*.

This is the kind of thinking that's in the air now. The story does stress human responsibility for the world, and this is good. But that's what makes it so difficult: it's all mixed up with the identity of God and the human self. In other words, here is an elite group of contemplatives who grock the future. This is fiction and it's silly. But it does reflect something very real. It tells us a great deal about where we stand in the modern world, about what we represent, about the fact that the world continues to look to contemplatives, not just for some marginal concern, but as central and essential. The novel recognizes this need for contemplatives, even though in a crazy way. The need for contemplatives is an ancient and genuine one, and it's still part of the picture.

Here's another interesting article about the primitive concept of vocation. First, it points out that a vocation can come along without someone intending it. You probably won't see where it's going to lead. This is because you're not just carrying out a function according to established norms but are feeling your way after new possibilities in ways of thinking and working. "One stage may open up another." This reminds us that a vocation is essentially open-ended, not something contained. Vocation is a creative possibility, leading to things we never suspected. Our job as communities and as individuals is to keep these possibilities wide open all the time, never to close down on vital potential. In our desire for security and for not having any trouble and for not being bothered by too many nitwit ideas, we've tended to close down on all ideas. Because there's been a lot of useless stuff that's a nuisance, we've more or less foreclosed on everything. But we've got to leave the possibilities open. It may be tiresome, but we need to try new things.

In Native American societies there are built-in rituals for young people. When a boy in an Indian tribe is reaching maturity and is going to become a man officially, he has to go through a difficult experience, usually with two or three others about the same age. He has to go out alone into some desolate and perilous place, up on a mountain, or on top of a cliff, or out in a canyon, with no food or human support. He has to mark out a certain area with a talisman here and there to show where the boundary is. Ideally he's got to stay there, fasting, until he has a vision. Most of the time it doesn't work, visions don't come that way. But he is supposed to come into contact with what is called his "vision-person," that is to say, not only his true self, his transcendent self, but almost what we would call his guardian angel, a spirit-being who will henceforth guide him in his hunting, his fighting, and everything. And he is under obedience to this spirit-being once he has seen it. This is tested by being referred back to the experienced elders of the tribe. It's all very serious.

Normally girls of the tribe do not go through this kind of thing unless they are going to be medicine women, a contemplative and prophetic elite in the tribe. A girl who is going to get involved in this is often a rather nervous type. It's taken for granted that if you are going to be a contemplative you are also going to be a very sensitive person.

You're likely to have trouble and go through all kinds of strange things that other people don't go through. I think we should remember this, because we are so set on having everybody "normal" in the convent that anyone slightly neurotic worries us. But you've got to be a little neurotic in this business! The girl has a rough time until she can accept her vocation, her destiny. It's akin to a deep religious conversion, one of the phenomena of adolescence. It frees a girl from her mother. The lesson of that is: there's no real freedom unless you go through a serious crisis which delivers you from dependence on other people. A person must have a certain distance from others; if not, there's no way to cross back over to another with anything to give. This is what we mean by getting out of symbiotic relationships, a sort of mass of confused people. Real giving requires a certain amount of distance so that one can come back across the gulf. Merely obliterating the gulf doesn't do it. It's a false community experience if there is no space between people. Lack of this distance causes serious problems.

So the young girl at first experiences great conflict. But this disappears when she surrenders to her vocation. Her conversion indicates that her psychic energy is now focused on new interests and tasks. She's self-possessed and dignified and her actions are "marked by charity." She is interested in people and has the power to allay and cure their ills. This experience of going through a testing or a crisis is good for the religious vocation, too. Making a decision and having one's energy organized around a real interest in life rules out the possibility of mediocrity. That there's always been this testing we can tell from primitive art, from the kind of drawings in caves. The people who did this were not only fantastic artists, they were obviously tremendous people. Their art is full of spiritual power. There's something contemplative about that which we cannot understand because they never had any writing.

Now it's time to ask again: Where do we look for the new thing? We look within ourselves. We have potentialities. The last text we looked at suggests that to develop these things there may have to be a crisis. People tend to get upset before taking a new step, and to feel isolated. We can help a little by being there and by being sympathetic, but it is very hard.

What about us? We're not here to be grocking and we're not shamans. Let's look at a familiar passage from Saint Paul in the light of what we've been hearing. We have to be attuned to what's going on in history and in ourselves, and we may have to go through a certain crisis. But who are we? We are just us, not imaginary people, just our flesh and blood selves. Paul says in I Corinthians [1:26-2:5]: "Take yourselves, brothers and sisters, at the time when you were called." The old version was "consider your vocation," this new one is better. We are still the same people as when God called us. Who was called when God called me? I am not somebody else, and never will be anybody else. "How many of you were wise in the ordinary sense of the word? How many were influential people or came from noble families?" I don't think we have a duke or duchess in the room! And we don't have to be wise. We just have to be ourselves. This contradicts the grocking thing. Life is not a question of a gnostic elite, of being especially smart, of being separated from everybody else. That is not us. On the contrary, we glory in our poverty and in our nothingness. We are poor sinners whom God has called to this particular kind of life.

"No, it was to shame the wise that God chose what is foolish by human reckoning, and to shame the strong that God chose what is weak by human reckoning." We are weak by human reckoning, and we remain so. We don't become miraculous beings. We make mistakes and do foolish things. "Those whom the world thinks common and contemptible are the ones that God has chosen." Therefore, it is not necessary to get mileage in the press and to become non-common and non-contemptible. Whether people like us or not doesn't really make much difference. We don't go around courting contempt, but if we're not admired, so what? We're not supposed to be admired by the world, nor do we need to be.

"The human race, those whom the world thinks common, are the ones whom God has chosen, those who are nothing at all to show up those who are everything. The human race has nothing to boast about to God. But you, God has made members of Christ Jesus, and by God's doing, Christ has become our wisdom and our virtue and our holiness and our freedom." Any good we have is not ours; it is Christ's. Understanding this is a key point in our lives, and never forgetting it. Because the joy and consolation of our life is realizing that what we have cannot be lost because it is God's. We can separate ourselves from it if we want to, but it is God's, and it is sure. That is our security. Not the security of I am a good person, I am a faithful religious. It is God who is good, whose mercy is without fail. If there is fidelity in my life, thank God. God is the one who does it, in spite of me.

There's no need to worry about these things. We just let Christ be faithful to us. If we live with that kind of mind, we are prophetic. We become prophetic when we live in such a way that our life is an experience of the infallible fidelity of God. That's the kind of prophecy we are called to, not the business of being able to smell the latest fashion coming ten years before it happens. It is simply being in tune with God's mercy and will.

"If anyone wants to boast, let it be about the Lord. As for me, when I came to you, it was not with any show of oratory or philosophy, but simply to tell you what God had guaranteed." This is prophetic. "During my stay with you, the only knowledge I claimed to have was about Jesus, and him crucified. Far from relying on any power of my own, I came among you in great fear and trembling. And in the speeches and sermons there were none of the arguments that belong to philosophy"— or grocking!—"but only a demonstration of the power of the spirit." In other words, if we trust God to act in us, God will act in us. This is how our lives become prophetic. Prophecy is not a technique, it is not about telling someone else what to do. If we are completely open to the Holy Spirit, then the Spirit will be able to lead us where God wants us to go. Going along that line, our lives will be prophetic.

It's so simple, and it's never been anything else. Renewal consists, above all, in recovering this truth. Everything else is accidental. Once we get on to this, everything else takes care of itself. We get into a lot of peripheral questions because we are too dominated by other people. As Paul says in Galatians, we have to maintain our own liberty. We must not allow ourselves to be dictated to by people who have no concept of what our life is about, and have no interest in it, and just want us to be like them. We've got no business being like anybody else. We're ourselves. Our only business is to be ourselves, to let God love us and save us with divine love and mercy. That's it.

Paul does, later on, talk about a wisdom for the perfect. What is this distinction? When he speaks of milk for the little ones, he refers to those who are still squabbling over incidentals like "I am of Apollos" or "I am of Paul." But we should not be getting that kind of baby food. Our vocation is to eat strong meat, to leave behind childish bickering and boasting.

Is Paul talking to individuals or to a community?

This letter is certainly addressed to the Church at Corinth, but I don't see any problem here. When Paul writes "you," he is surely talking to individuals as well as to the community. Community is not a fixed reality or an ideal that one is drawn to like a magnet. It is created by the interaction of the individual people who make it up.

And the community is the best interpreter of its own inner life, not the Superior.

Of course. But people in community have not always been articulate enough; this is one of the things that we have to do now. The mind of the community should not be dictated by something from outside itself. We do have a way to go here.

The very attitude of the individuals in community is part of the creative force of the community.

Yes, and it's a question, too, of our presence to one another and our response to one another. The reality of community is created by a real presence of the members to one another as persons, by genuine exchange among themselves. If that doesn't occur, there are serious problems. Members have to confront one another as persons, and if there's a fight, *they* have to work it out, not the superior. Rosemary Haughton's book, *The Transformation of Man,* deals with this very well. She is the mother of ten children and shows how this in-fighting is something like what happens with youngsters. It's a way of really finding out who we are as persons. Theology really happens in relations between people. And if theology is bad from poor interpersonal relations and this is written down somewhere and put on a shelf for future reference, we're in trouble. I'm willing to admit that poor relating is and can be a great problem in communities.

We often find that when we get into mutual exchange among ourselves, we theorize too much or we bump into the law or the Rule, and we get stymied. For instance, in matters pertaining to cloister or communication with persons outside.

I don't think there are insuperable canonical problems with these things. And there is nothing stopping you from growth in interpersonal relationships in the community. You *can* function there. It seems to me that persons from other convents should be able to come in and visit for a while. We have never had any problem about that in our order. Monks generally can move from one monastery to another without much difficulty. If there are difficulties, that has to be changed. When something is blocking religious life, you have not only a right but an obligation to change it. But you have to do it with care.

Would you say something about pushing a little beyond the law?

We have to, we have to. This is not only permissible but there is a time when it's necessary. It's understood that no law covers all eventualities, and especially at a time like this when so much is up in the air. Most laws fall short. A law can block unreasonably, or it can simply not apply in the way it is written. When this is the case, it is an act of virtue to break through it and attain the end for which the law was obviously instituted. For example, the purpose of the law of enclosure is ultimately to ensure the kind of development that we have been talking about. It's supposed to promote that. If this law reaches the point where it's stifling development and no longer fulfilling its purpose, then it is meaningless.

Contemporary Prophetic Choices

Let's talk a little about choices. Almost everyone in our society today would like to see us out of Vietnam, would like the war to stop, but no one is in a position to make that happen just by a personal decision. The only kind of choice that people can make that may or may not have significance is the one that Dan Berrigan made, which is totally unpopular and incomprehensible. What he is actually saying, consciously or unconsciously, is that our society is really a kind of jail. And in such a society you might as well be in jail, because you're not free outside. But often, people do not understand these drastic and symbolic choices.

I'm not saying that we have to make that kind of choice. But we're in a society where everything is so predetermined that being prophetic is simply not going to fit anybody's preconceived ideas. The contemplative life will not be applauded if it becomes prophetic. It's going to be condemned even more than it is already. Nevertheless younger people are definitely open to it, and will be ready for it. They sense what their elders don't. They believe that religious life and contemplative life should have something of this prophetic awareness. They're looking around to discover if others are conscious of the situation. Many of them write to ask if the Abbey of Gethsemani is this sort of place. It isn't, but it could be. Here, as everywhere else, we are shortsighted and don't know enough about the world we are living in. Some monks feel that it's enough to live a more or less authentic and somewhat updated life. That's not enough, there's no future in that. The mere fact of living an honest life that is also a little bit human may tide us over until we die. There's nothing wrong with it, but in our hearts we know that's not what we're called to. We have to be more than sincere people of prayer.

We have a prophetic task. We have to rock the boat, but not like the hippies. Herbert Marcuse claims that even when you rock the boat you are meeting the demands of a totalitarian society, which requires a certain number of boat-rockers. A good magazine needs to have a few pages in each issue about people who are stirring up things, who look funny to others. We could easily fulfill that role! A group of nuns performs a dance after Mass and it's very beautiful, very prayerful. But if the *National Catholic Reporter* gets hold of it, every reader believes that something really different and very exciting has happened, and that it will have to be stopped. But nothing will have happened at all.

We're conditioned for this kind of thing, and it's a problem. But we have to go beyond just doing something new that creates a stir and a lot of comment. It's just froth, part of the system, a small beginning. Such gestures can be exhausting, but there's no way to avoid them.

There is more to being prophetic than that. Look at the Gospel of Mark, which scholars say is a desert gospel. The idea of the temptation in the desert runs all through this gospel. It's a prelude to the Passion, making the whole Gospel of one piece. Remember that the temptation in the desert centers on power, among other things. "I will give you all these kingdoms *if* . . . " The real reply to that is the Crucifixion. The prophetic struggle with the world is the struggle of the Cross against worldly power.

For centuries the Church has been involved in worldly power. The Church is, in fact, a worldly power. The great problem of contemplative life, of religious life, of the priesthood and of everyone else, is that we have been corrupted by that power. We have been used by this structure to justify a power politics in the Church. Any arguments about the essence of contemplative life that come down on the conservative side tend to point that way. Contemplatives are seen, *par excellence,* as people who accept what comes from above, without question. We have become the people who worship and justify this power: "Look at these holy, humble people. They know our power comes from God." We could be participating in one of the great forms of idol worship. Not deliberately, but that could be interpreted as what we're involved in.

Certainly the things we go through in good faith, the kinds of things we've done in the name of obedience, and the sacrifices we've made are not lost for us as individuals. God takes everything into account. But it isn't helping the Church; it may even be hindering it. We've got to consider that. If we're going to take our prophetic vocation seriously, we have to see this aspect of it. God will surely protect a person who obeys out of goodwill. But this doesn't mean that it's going to do the Church any good.

The young don't think that way.

No, no. It would be such a good thing if somebody would tell the people at the other end—the leaders—that this is the situation. It's very hard to convince them of this, because they regard the problem as temporary.

They haven't even come to the idea of compromise yet, let alone our going ahead.

People in authority have educated themselves to a certain way of thinking, so they are caught in a terrible bind. It's a vicious circle. "It's not a matter of opinion, it's a matter of truth, this is of faith, this is of God." And that stops all dissent, there is no place for discussion or argument. Anyone who differs is a heretic.

What can you say against that?

There's no argument. It isn't a question of what you think, or what I think; this is God, this is the faith, this is it. This is the position of people who are scared, who don't dare question anything. I once saw a Charlie Chaplin movie where Charlie is sitting with this blind girl he likes very much and she's knitting. Somehow a thread from his underwear gets caught and it all begins to unravel. So it's like that. They're afraid. If you start pulling on one thread, pretty soon . . .

. . . *you'll lose your underwear!*

In this situation, prophets are not acceptable. They have to question everything. It's essential that we realize what the situation is and see some of its implications. "They will throw you out of the synagogues and put you to death." I know where I stand and where I don't. I'll go along with official people as long as I can, but many of the people I'm in tune with—like artists, philosophers, and scientists—are outside the Church. It seems to me that even the progressive voices, Christians among them, are still more or less just Great Society liberals. They have an optimism that basically accepts the status quo, and they are not all that different from those who are fearful. They offer some good insights and new images, but for the most part, they're happy, not alienated, and think our society is good and really going somewhere. What they say is useless. In reality, they see no alternative.

There is another choice. We don't have to follow anybody's line. We don't have to choose either nineteenth-century conservatism or one of the two brands of progressive ideas, liberal or Marxist. These are not expressly political, but there's a sort of political orientation behind them. People who take on a Marxist type of approach, like some of the French Catholics, no matter how sharp their social criticism is, really end up in a political structure. For these people, the prophetic life and the radical Christian life and the eschatological life lead only to revolution. But it's not a free choice. What they are doing is accepting a choice dictated by Marxist ideology. It's not like the Russian situation at all, it's very French. So I think we have to be very careful of the people who simply equate the prophetic choice with the Marxist choice. That's very easy for a certain kind of Christian to do—not American Christians so much as Latin American and French and Italian Christians.

There's a sort of biblical mystique behind Marx. He has an eschatology and a dynamic sense of history, along with a "chosen people" idea. The biblical revival can even provide a few snap arguments to support his thinking, which fit in nicely with what some are thinking. You get the feeling that Marx was a real Moses figure. In a certain sense he felt himself to be that. The imagery of the Exodus is everywhere in Marx, and although his ideology is based on economics, the symbolism is clear. For certain progressive Catholics, this provides the answer. But here again, it's too easy, it's been predetermined by somebody else.

But take, for example, the person of Che Guevara. Why is this man such a popular symbol? For one thing, he inspired the young. Within days after he was killed, a group of young poets in London wrote and said they were publishing a commemorative volume for Che from poets around the world. It was a spontaneous action. Che didn't really achieve anything, but he did lay his life on the line and that was a heroic thing. He fought in the jungle, not on TV; he was outside the structure. He was not identified with any particular nation because he was Argentinean but went to fight in Cuba and Venezuela and Bolivia. A mystery man, a kind of prophet. This is what's great about him. He fulfilled the desire for a prophet that many young people always have.

Malcolm X is similar. His whole life was a fight against society. He began as a black man completely dominated by the system. He fitted into the system by becoming a pseudo-rebel; that is, he lived outside the law. But to be outside the law is to be cooperating with the society that needs deviants. Therefore, while he was outside, he was still part of the machine, still playing the games that many politicians and businessmen play. He was finally caught in the machine and went to jail, where he was converted to the Muslims. That doesn't work too well, either. It was the pilgrimage to Mecca that really made the difference. Before that he had a very naive and absolute anti-white bias. In Mecca he discovered that color doesn't matter that much, that people are of many colors, that they are brothers and sisters anyway in a single world community. He came home to his own people and was shot.

There's prophetic typology here: Malcolm liberated himself from the system, began making choices from his own center, and redeemed the meaning of "soul." Malcolm had soul. "Soul" has became a bad word for us, but it's a good word for his people. A good book is a soul book.

Malcolm X discovered a world community, he chose his own community. That's a very important thing. After that, he went around to many African states, meeting new brothers and sisters. Earlier, he had spent a long time working in Roxbury. Had he not been killed, he would have become a great man. He and Che show us what the prophetic formula is. If we cannot be like that, we should at least be followers of people like that. A Malcolm X or a Che should be able to take refuge in a Carmel.

Martin Luther King, Jr., too, is a hero for everybody. But he was much more involved with the establishment. He was a wonderfully good man who had to deal with the political aspect of the machine and sometimes got caught in it. The disagreement between him and the black radicals seems to be the reason why he decided to go ahead, even with the expectation of being killed. It seems he had reached the point of a showdown and that he had to vindicate his whole vocation and existence by putting his life on the line. And he did. Possibly it was the only thing he could do.

He obviously knew his death was imminent.

Yes, he had clearly accepted it. He may have felt that it was one last thing he could do that was not equivocal. This is a kind of pattern of what's required for the prophetic vocation. Not that we have to go out and get shot, but that we have to have a clear grasp of the situation and be unequivocal about it. It may mean that sooner or later we will be faced with choices which require a break with the establishment. In the meantime, we go along with the assumption that, as much as we can, we'll try to work within the structures and save what we have for the sake of the people we are with. We also have to be careful that we are not doing all this ourselves. It has to be God. We are not Malcolm X or anyone else. What we do may be small, or in small groups—that's okay.

These examples are good because they demonstrate

ways of being prophetic. It's a temptation to think that the whole story is in the peace movement, or the civil rights movement, or any other kind of movement. My criticism of people in movements is not that they're trying to be heroic or prophetic but that they seem to have put all their eggs in one basket. Political protest in the long run helps the system. Like the protest of the young man who burned himself alive. Some people tried to say this was prophetic. It wasn't—it was absurd. He didn't know what he was doing. Seeing a thing like that, a lot of people who were undecided are going to make up their minds in favor of patriotism.

What about burning draft cards or records?

That's a big problem. Definitely, it's an attack on authority, an aggressive act. It's also, in some way, a violent act; it's not intended to be non-violent. I admire the integrity of some people I know who do that, but I will not say that that's exactly what I'd do. I think it's going to help the draft, because an act like that tends to scare people into obeying the draft law rather than encouraging them to resist. It raises the issue in such a way that people get confused and afraid.

These are exceptional acts which people do for their own reasons. All we can do is respect their conscience and go along with it as far as we can. For myself, I agree that the Vietnam War and the draft are immoral because our country is not really threatened. There is no national emergency. Our young men are dying as victims of the political power of leaders and for the interests of those behind the war. It's a tragic thing. If a fellow thinks he should go, that's his conscience. But if he doesn't, he should resist.

What about destroying public property, like records?

I think someone can do that in good conscience if it seems right. But I don't think it's effective communication because it antagonizes people.

I was talking to a Japanese woman on the plane about the Vietnam War and she said that quite a number of people she talks to don't want the war to end. For instance, one manufacturer in Hong Kong said they were making all kinds of corpse bags for the dead bodies.

This is terrible, unthinkable. A lot of our own military are making a lot of money on the black market, too, selling American cigarettes and whiskey and other things. People soft-pedal this corruption and sweep it under the rug. Think of the number of Vietnamese girls who are prostitutes as a result of this war. And all the innocent children who are getting burned up. If you say such things, it's called propaganda—but it's true.

Is there anything the Vietnamese can do in all this to help themselves in some way?

Nhat Hanh, a Buddhist monk, is trying to do this. He went all over the country trying to tell people that neither the Vietcong nor the Saigon government really represented the Vietnamese people. All the common people know is that they're being bombed. A few years ago, when it was still possible to do something, they wanted to have a kind of political coalition of their own, all the sides getting together to try to run their own affairs. They were supposed to be allowed to do this. But the government was afraid that it wouldn't be voted in, so the election was completely rigged.

Do you think the Communist government is any worse than what the French did to the Vietnamese?

It could be. I don't know. The Vietcong is no Sunday school; Asian Communism is no joke. But what the French did was bad. People have a right to run their own affairs. There's no reason why Vietnam has to have the kind of government that will please us. If Communism spreads all over Asia and the Asians themselves want it, that's their business. We have no right to tell a country what kind of government it has to have. Some might say that the Communists are forcing themselves upon the people. But the more the war goes on, the more the people decide that their only hope is with the Vietcong, because things couldn't be any worse than what they have.

Respect for Each Person, Diversity in Community

We were talking before about people needing different things, about this pull between some who want more activity and some who want more contemplation. So communities are feeling this pull in two directions. How possible is it to give everyone a chance to go in opposite directions? Can you expand each way or is it too much? Is it going to harm the place?

Only time will tell. It might depend on the size of the community.

Here we wouldn't have much trouble. But these differences might disrupt a small community. In our case, I would say, talking without any of the responsibilities of the abbot, instead of all these people getting dispensations, the abbot might be able to turn them loose for a year or two if they have special needs. For more activity, they might go to the Taize brothers in Chicago. There's a Franciscan there now. Let anybody who wants to see what real poverty looks like go there, instead of having to start something from scratch or having to leave the order. Then they could come back later.

Do you think it's usual in a vocation to reach a point where you feel you need to be freer?

Everybody goes through phases of wanting more of this and that. I think there should be a way of letting people have more freedom without their having to leave the order. They could go out temporarily, and still feel part of the community. The question of discernment of spirits comes up here. It's not a matter of people simply doing what they please.

One Superior of a cloistered community circulated a letter to find out what others thought about permitting sisters to go to active communities for a time. I think she was looking at the need some sisters have for a change of environment.

They need to get out—why? If people have serious problems, we shouldn't dump them onto another community. It's always a temptation, when someone is a burden, to send him or her somewhere else and see if that works. We have to make a distinction between people who have problems and people who simply have a need for releasing tensions, which often come from being too far out of touch with reality. It's all too easy just to chew and chew on nothing and to spend all kinds of time trying to figure out something when there's nothing to figure out. If they can just get in contact with people who have real problems, they can forget themselves and things will straighten out easily.

But the pluralism that I had in mind is the possibility of people doing all kinds of things within the limits of each community. How far that could go would be up to the community to decide.

The thing that puzzles me about this is that it seems the basic aims of the community would have to be extremely broad and general, like "We're here to seek God."

There would have to be a very solid nucleus of people really wanting the same thing in order to support this alternative. There can't be a community at all if everybody is going in all directions at once.

We have enough people in the active communities who think they could solve their problems by going into a cloistered community. But that usually lasts only a few months before they find out that the problem doesn't lie in the type of life but in something else.

The only benefit of the change I can see is that a change of perspective comes when a person really sees she's not on

*top of her problems. The new situation might help reveal
what the need really is, or it may bring on a change that
wouldn't have happened otherwise. I question people having to be in the same mold. We have people who don't
seem very prayerful, but sometimes they are the best people in the community.*

Sure. We've got at least half the community here like that,
if not more. And often they are much better humanly, more
charitable than others who want to pray. Actually, I would
say that the rule of Saint Benedict is very flexible. It presupposes that a person, without even thinking about it,
even while going on exteriorly as a more or less active person, can become a very interior person without even
realizing it.

*We can't really say that these people who look like they
don't pray, don't.*

That's right; they are prayerful, but they're also less self-
conscious doing it. For any religious, self-forgetfulness is a
real litmus test. If a person is self-conscious at prayer, that
will become problematic. This is one of the problems with a
deliberately sought, solitary prayer life. Given an unlimited
amount of time to be alone, a person is apt to explode in a
short time. On the other hand, if people are more or less self-
forgetful, they are probably in the right place, they are
where they belong. If you take one of those good community persons you talked about and make her sit down and try
to pray, she will most likely get upset and unhappy.

On the other hand, there's another type of person who,
if thrown into activity, becomes extremely self-conscious.
People like this worry about everything they do. They are
scrupulous, get easily upset, and feel they make a mess of
things. But if they just let themselves do something simple,
they are quite happy. This is part of the real formation of our
life. So it seems to me that self-forgetfulness is the key. A
great deal goes on without the person knowing it.

But before you get to that stage, where you can transcend

yourself, you must know yourself, who you are, with all your limitations. You have to love yourself very well and realize that you are loved, in order to have a good self-concept. Then you can transcend it.

This is very true. You can't forget yourself if you're constantly trying to justify your relations with other people. Self-justification is really a matter of not wanting to believe that you are loved. If I do not believe I am loved, I'm going to want to be justified. If no one else justifies me, I will justify myself, usually by trying to dominate everyone else. This is the bane of everything. When you're confident that you are loved, you have no need to show God or anyone else why you *should* be loved. You do not have to justify yourself.

That's why we have to be psychologically mature before we can be spiritually mature.

That's right. The whole love situation in families today is so undermined and attacked. Parents tend to doubt their love for one another much more now, because they are constantly being bombarded by advertising with its diabolical implication that, in order to be a lovable person, you have to use all the products. This is one of the most hateful things that can be done to a person and it's happening all the time. It's dreadful because people cannot resist it, and so keep getting caught. We have to watch out for this, too, because we've had the same kind of thing with the old legalism: If you don't do such and such, you aren't worthy of love. If you can't measure up to the requirements, you won't be loved. This is the great tyranny that people automatically use to make others feel unloved, because they don't measure up. It's a way of saying "We're in, and you're not.'

Receiving love from others is the quickest way for a person to grow.

And not only love, but also respect. Respect is essential to love but it can be lost sight of. Often, young people are very doubtful about themselves. They think that what they really want is the affective side of love. But really, respect is what they want first, although they wouldn't admit it.

To esteem a person precisely as that person is what counts. Just to love a person because she is who she is, or he is who he is, and not for any other reason, is genuine support. We don't love others for what they do or don't do. No one has to pay for being esteemed. You don't have to make some sort of grade. If all the talk about freedom doesn't presuppose this, it's a lie or it's suspect. People may be odd or different, and even have screwy ideas. Still, each one is worthy of respect. They don't need to fit into some sort of classification before they are respected.

With racism, it is the same. We try to make people "measure up." With a little more subtlety, you can also classify people according to their political opinions and other things. For us, it all comes down to the gospel: "Judge not." One of the important things about spiritual formation is to train people not to judge, to teach them not to box others in. It's easy in religious life just to live on the constant activity of judging and classifying others, putting people in their places, mentally keeping them down.

Gradually we come to see that these different boxes or categories do not matter at all, they have nothing to do with the essence of life. That's why we can be hopeful. We don't have to build some great big new thing and then defend from scratch. If we can get this nonsense about judging and about literal perfection in every little thing out of the way, then what's real can emerge. When we let our boxes go, we'll find the real thing is there. Just the fact that we are human beings will, with the grace of God, be enough.

The value of people is just so great. It's true that our society has made some things a bit tough for us. But it's also done a lot for us. If we'd grown up in a primitive society, we probably never would have made it to our present age. We would have died in infancy or before we were fifteen years old. There are some fantastic statistics that indicate about half the people who have ever existed on earth have lived within the last century. A certain kind of eschatological feeling comes when we see that the human race is really us. And also when we realize that half the population is under twenty-five.

That's another thing about our culture. It's aimed at youth and if you don't qualify, you feel kind of "guilty."

This is another insidious thing, because, in fact, the young people themselves are being exploited. For example, in the drug business, even though some of it is coming from the new generation, a lot of it is dealers and other people who are contaminating the lesser drugs with habit-forming drugs, so the younger people get hooked on an expensive drug without even knowing it. They're often helpless, but all the time they think they're running a whole independent operation. Some extremely vicious and smart people are not averse to making a great deal of money out of the whole situation. Then the media picks it all up and romanticizes the issue. This is tragic.

Young people have such a need to be accepted and can so easily latch on to what seems the smartest thing going. They're not able to defend themselves.

Yes, and they're really good. We ought to be able to help them in some way, but there's not much we can do. We can certainly listen when they come to us. Often in their honest but misguided way, they are looking for something that has experiential meaning. In another time, they might well have been among the ones coming to our convents and monasteries. If things had been a little different, they might be coming our way instead of going the way of drugs.

Young people today believe that if all that is said about religion is true, if God is real, then there must be some way of experiencing that truth. And if God can be experienced, why shouldn't there be a shortcut? Someone comes along and says yes, there is a shortcut, so they try it and conclude it's an experience of God. I think we've all had the equivalent of an LSD trip. I used to get it from *real coffee* in the old days! All you need is a kind of high. But this is not contemplation at all. It's the kind of trip you go on when you hit choir one day, and you're really keyed up, and everything just kind of bursts into flame, the whole place is rocking! This is more normal for novices in the beginning of religious life. We can all remember times like that.

I'm reminded of something I read about Teresa of Avila, that at one time she had a much higher gift of prayer than she had virtues.

Actually, gifts of prayer don't have to be tied up with levels of virtue. What they do need to be tied up with is goodwill. If a person has a great deal of goodwill, then the achievement isn't the important thing, the goodwill is. The sincerity and the honest intending are what matter. This is clear with the saints. You cannot find a saint who wasn't severely criticized. None of them was thought to be what they all were supposed to be. One of the very holy men of our order was Dom Lehodey, who wrote a book called *Holy Abandonment*. He had been through terrible suffering and was dying in the infirmary. One of the brothers heard him moaning and chewed him out: "What are you doing, complaining like this? And people think you're a saint!" This is unbelievably inhuman, the old French school.

A lot of trouble for some people in our kind of life consists in the fact that they're never able to express themselves honestly about anything. They can't say what they think. There's been a discussion group here that gave people who felt as if they were never consulted a chance to air their views and disagree. There was a big blowup, but after that, much more acceptance of things and much better feelings. It's rough to have things going on and not feel a part of them, or to feel that others don't care what you think about anything.

Just to know you can strongly disagree with the group and it's perfectly all right.

That's why superiors need to know something about this. The transference involved is very difficult and exhausting, and we really don't have the training for it. We simply experience an encounter with someone who's extremely unreasonable. You can't quite understand why, and you just have to put up with it. If the person were angry with you it would be easier, but in reality, it's an anger against someone else, maybe a parent or some person you have no way of knowing. So there's no way to communicate, to know the proper emotional response. A psychiatrist has freely taken this on and has learned to accept this transference and knows how to respond. But even then, it's exhausting. Still, it's a relief to know that this anger, at least for the most part, is really not directed at you.

This takes away the sense of a personal attack.

That's right. We have to understand that neurotics prefer to suffer, because this enables them to live through the situation that they've never moved beyond. They're trapped. And so they constantly fall back into the suffering which has caused their pain. This gives them some sense of reality, the only kind they have. Therefore they use other people to put themselves in this suffering kind of position. If you play along with this, you get riled up, and they love it. Only by going through analysis yourself can you understand the machinery of it.

The more emotionally involved we get, the more we augment the whole thing.

Sure, sure. Really, there ought to be more honest praise for the efforts made to cope with these problems. There's very little recognition in our lives Even when someone dies, it's understood that you don't give it too much attention; there's maybe a passing allusion to the fact that so and so was once around! But it's good to give people recognition for what they do. Not just a routine acknowledgment, either, although this can be okay, too. We need it.

It's Paul Ricoeur who says that we all need more recognition than we get.

This gets us back to how important it is to esteem one another.

Then, why don't we? There are so many other things we think are more important than listening to others or giving them time. We think we could be using our time much better. Well, we couldn't. We need the conviction that we can't do better than to love someone in a simple, non-productive sort of way. In our society you have to produce, period. Being kind to someone or sympathetic, we think, is not getting anything done. This gets pretty close to being one of the real tests.

In an old form of asceticism it was considered a fault if somebody praised you.

Maybe people were tougher then. With men, the idea of not praising anybody goes back to the old patriarchal society, where nobody can rival Dad. And, of course, women don't even enter the picture! Maybe it's also a kind of magic reaction, a kind of superstition that you better watch out if you let yourself be praised, the old superstitious mentality of retribution. There's always a great deal of that around. This is pre-Christian. We have to recognize what Paul means when he says we are not under the law, that the fact of being praised is not bad luck. There might be some psychological justification for not being praised, maybe a person would be less cautious and get out of step. But as Christians we no longer live according to that philosophy of life in which the individual ego is the center of everything. So if my ego is menaced by a fall, maybe there's good in that. We don't have to worry about it that much. If I do fall on my face, I pick myself up and go on. It's okay.

But, on the other hand, we do need praise. It's not good for us to fall on our face, and we have to take that into account. Basically, we have to deal with a mixture of motives, non-Christian motives, ego motives, pagan motives, superstitious motives. There are plenty of all these in our racial and ethnic backgrounds. And we carry them with us. But, as Christians, we constantly try to rise above these things. Our only real justification is the freedom of the children of God.

Psychologically, we have to take into account that there's always yes and no in everything that we do. We're like an iceberg with a certain amount above the surface and an enormous amount under the surface. At the very moment I say, "I'm going to be holy," there's another I that says, "I'm going to be unholy." If I'm not a well-integrated person, if my resolution to be holy has a lot of mixed motives without my knowing it, then it is all the more likely that, in the things I do to be holy, I am going to be, at the same time, defeating myself. I'm going to trip myself up in my very efforts to be holy.

It's the same with prayer. We want a deep life of prayer, and we don't want a deep life of prayer. We would like to be united with God, and we would like not to be united with God. It's very difficult to pray when you're terribly earnest about it; it's much easier when you're not so earnest and when you're not making resolutions to be a great soul of prayer. The part of you which doesn't want to do these things and which you have suppressed works against you.

So when we make up our minds to do certain things, we are also, without realizing it, putting ourselves in positions where we frustrate ourselves and don't do what we ought to do. Here again, as Christians, we should not be that religious. It's love that gets us beyond religiosity. There's all the difference in the world between what happens with my unconscious mechanism when I am loving and what happens when I am not loving. All love involves hate; there's no such thing as an absolutely unmixed human love. There is a yes and a no, the positive and the negative. But if real love is there, the elements of resistance and hate and rejection are much less. That's why it's so important to be doing things out of love. A certain element of resistance will be there, but since I'm not straining to make something work, it will be easier to deal with it.

Self-forgetfulness comes in here. We work much better when we're oriented to another person. We have to remember that, when we're talking about our psychophysical machinery, and quite apart from the fuss about fulfillment, the way a human being functions best, ideally, is when united with a person of the opposite sex. This is our normal condition. I'm not speaking in terms of problems, because modern married life is complicated and rough and it's a lot simpler to be celibate. But when two people are very much in love with each other, this business of carrying one another's burdens is immensely simplified. Of course, it wears off and gets rough again. The rare people who have had the wonderful experience of being happily married for a lifetime give witness to the fact that this is the way we are naturally meant to live. But many people can't make it.

Why do we have this idea that if a thing is harder it's better?

A person with a certain type of mentality may feel more secure if things are a little hard. This is okay. When things are hard, it's a challenge, and challenge can be good for us. We like it and need it.

We need it as a proof of love?

We need it as a stimulus of love. The challenge brings out love. We have to be called on to pay a little bit for what we're doing. In that sense, I think it's normal and healthy to think that when a thing is hard, it's good. This idea is not necessarily masochistic, provided what is involved is human and reasonable. It must not be self-punishing. Life would get pretty bad without any challenge, without our coming up against any kind of obstacle. What kind of life would that be?

Well, these things are complicated and there are many sides to them. But basically, there is a kind of cycle of going through periods of meeting opposition and paying the price, and then knowing love and consolation when we can coast a little. Back and forth, that's the way it has to be. We need to be realistic about it all, we can't help defeating ourselves to some extent. We need to put our trust in God. God sees us through, things don't have to be working perfectly all the time. There are long periods, too, when we're just in a sort of semi-stupor. We shouldn't expect unrealistic things of ourselves.

In our lives, it seems that challenges are mostly concerned with ourselves.

Yes, we try to prove ourselves to ourselves. There's no need to justify, really. One thing about this meeting that keeps coming to me these days: just the fact that you people are you is good enough. And the fact that you've been able to be here and to share. If we hadn't done anything, it would still be of great value just that you were here. God has given us something in these four days that can never be taken away. We are different and our lives are changed. And it wasn't hard!

Most things in the Christian life are that way. If we trust God, this is the way God likes to act. The simplicity of our encounter brings with it the authentic mark of grace. This is comforting because we know that that's going to come around again in all sorts of various ways. When you get back home, you're reassured that that stamp of simplicity will be upon what happens in your own community, no matter how complex things get. The normal thing is this simplicity, the fact that we have seen and tasted that the Lord is good. We need to thank God for that.

We need to thank you, too!

I'm grateful to you, too, because you've given me an enormous amount. I frankly think that the men and women of contemplative orders need much more communication between them. This isn't the Middle Ages. A lot could be done with more brother-and-sister sharing. We have to realize that contemplatives are very much the same on both sides of the gender fence. Men contemplatives should be in a position to appreciate the values of women more. You have to remember that men are jealous of women, as you probably know if you've had brothers. I think one of the problems of the American male today is that he is terrified of women. He constantly has to hit women over the head to prove he's boss. Advertising also ties into this imaging business, the macho male. But it seems to me that men in contemplative life should not necessarily have that drawback.

So, let's pray. O Lord, we thank you from the bottom of our hearts for the grace and mercy and love that you have shown us in these days, and we beg you to help us live up to this, not by any great deeds of ours, but by continuing to trust, and continuing to be grateful, and continuing to look to you in all things for the kind of simplicity and grace that you have shown us these days. Through Christ our Lord.

Amen.

Honesty in Choosing Life, Union with God

(Following Mass at the Hermitage, December 7, 1967)

This morning I was thinking again about community and contemplation and how simple it is. There's a good twelfth-century Cistercian text that relates this with the Trinity. The writer says that the Son in us loves the Father through the Spirit. This is the key to both community and contemplation. God in each one of us, no one ever an object, and the Word, the subject in me who loves you. And you are not object, either. An interpersonal relationship is never a subject-object relationship.

The subject in me loves the subject in you, and there you have, so to speak, one being in two persons. The Cistercian says that community life in a monastery is nothing but an extension of the inner life of the Trinity, and that the relationship between us as persons is a relationship like that between the divine persons. The Holy Spirit in each one of us makes us love one another. The other is not an object out there but my other self. You are not distracted by yourself unless it's your false self. People are not a distraction unless they are falsified, made into an object.

My idea of solitude is false if I have to withdraw from every human being in the world because they're all objects. Then everything in the world is a distraction. Another word for that is hell. This reminds me of my friend Will Campbell, the one who preaches to the KKK "because they need to be converted," he says. Well, Will needs an operation and his doctor, who's completely against integration, gets him under the knife. Will's wife says, "Be careful with my husband. No monkey business." Will comes out of the operation with a terribly sore shoulder and can't understand why it hurts, because the surgery was on his stomach. The doctor says, "A funny thing happened on the table. Your heart stopped. We used to call that death." And so they had to massage his heart. Afterward, talking to Will's wife, the doctor says, "When that guy's heart stopped, I thought of you, and what you had told me. And I thought, 'They've got me for sure this time—I *won't* let him die.'"

Anyway, the point in being by yourself is not to run away from everybody in the world. That makes no sense at all. You don't have to run away from them or run to them. Being alone is just another way of being with them. The question of being physically present to everybody is more or less irrelevant most of the time. Either you are or you aren't. It doesn't make that much difference, because we are united in Spirit. And that's what it's going to be in heaven. In heaven there's a real common life without any of the nonsense. We're not worried about our own identity and our own selfhood and all of that.

In heaven it will be the way it is when it's best for us on earth, and much better. In other words, we will really be one. That's what our life is about, what we're looking for, and what we're going to have. We will overcome, we will be free, we will be one. We don't have to worry about the fact that it's only imperfect now. It's coming, and it will be much better than we could possibly think or imagine. It will be that way because of one another. So we have made our eternity better by these four days together. That's what Christianity is. That's the way God works. And that's what makes us so grateful. We know we don't have to make anything "work" or fulfill some kind of precondition, or get everything "right."

Today I came across an article about progress and regress in history. It says something new and I think it makes a good point. It starts with the idea of means and ends. In the normal succession of things that we deal with every day, the ends are implied in the means. For example, if you want to use a hammer, you don't sit down and put the hammer on the table and meditate on it. You pick it up and drive a nail into the wall. When you're driving the nail into the wall, you're not thinking about the hammer, you're thinking about getting the nail in the wall. Later on, you'll hammer another nail, and so on. One thing naturally leads to another. This is an "ordinary succession of things." This is the way things normally progress, which implies making use of the means that you have toward the ends that are built into the means.

Now, we all realize and have observed that, in our modern world, instead of having a means which leads to an end, you start something first. Then you invent an end to justify why you're doing it. A rich man starts a foundation because he wants his millions to be tax-exempt, then he finds a purpose for the foundation. This gets to be more and more of a pattern. Instead of having ends, you are reflecting back on the means all the time. This leads to the means becoming the end. So means become sort of autonomous, they work by themselves.

I think the relevance of this is clear. We're liable to do this very thing in religious change, to get distracted from the fact that we have real ends to attain and that there's a normal progression toward them. We can fall into one of those vicious circles where life just goes round and round without getting anywhere. We start doing something and then invent a reason to justify doing it. Think of some of the implications of this. The Vietnam War is in our minds all the time. And it strikes me that a lot of the wars we have now are wars that somebody has started to prove that we ought to have a war, to prove that war is necessary. Or, as Simone Weil put it, you start a war and a thousand soldiers are killed. After that, you're committed. You have to go back and fight some more, because these thousand dead will haunt you if you don't go and avenge them. This is an illustration of original sin, the way it gets into the whole war picture. This article develops the idea further and says that maybe the reason people stop going forward and start going back is that they're already near the end and they really don't want to reach it. For example, world peace is now possible, it's in sight. With a bit more effort and a bit more sense, we could have it. Leaders may be backtracking into wars on all sides because we just don't know how to cope with peace.

This may be the way it is with us in our lives. Maybe the end is much closer than we think. Nobody can really stop us. There is such a thing as rebellion in order to justify submission. This is an adolescent trait. We see it in kids: a teenager who fights because he wants to be slapped down—he's never been slapped down before so he starts a fight to make it happen. Then he has a grievance for fighting some more and the cycle is repeated.

Sometimes, in our attitude toward authorities—who can be a nuisance, it's true—we can do this. But we don't have to get into that kind of bind. Maybe the ends are much closer to us than we realize. The way we've been together here shows us that all the qualities are there. We lack nothing. We are the most favored people on the face of the earth, except for a few trimmings that are kind of irritating but can't be helped. Who has ever had the chances that we have, the breaks that we've had? What we want may be right there. Maybe what we need to do is just simply go and get it and not become involved in some kind of machinery for fighting somebody who may try to stop us from getting our ends. There'd be no need to complain then, "They won't let us be contemplative, or they won't let us do this or that." This could be an issue, I don't know. Let's open the discussion.

People come to us and ask us to teach them about contemplative prayer. And it's hard even to talk about. What would be your ideas on what we could give them?

Well, there's got to be a completely Zen-like approach. When you ask a Zen master, "What is the meaning of Zen?"

he hits you over the head, or something like that, and then leaves you to think about it for a while. Under no circumstance will you ever get a lecture on Zen. On something else, yes, but not on Zen.

When the Sufi fellow came to visit here—the one I told you about, who's a real mystic and very down-to-earth—we had some sessions with him. One of our most earnest monks and perhaps a future abbot asked him, "How do you attain union with God?" What are the means, how do you do it, what's the system? The Sufi just laughed and said, "We don't answer questions like that." He passed it off, wouldn't have anything to do with it. You don't answer questions like that, because there's only one answer. And that is, union with God.

Zen people stress the fact that if you weren't such a dope, you'd know that you are united to God, that God is already that close. So all right, somebody comes and asks about contemplative prayer. The thing to do is, somehow or other, taking into consideration their person and background, to get them into a position where they're capable of realizing how close God is. Buddhist teaching says the only thing standing in the way is ignorance. But this ignorance is tied up with everything else.

The root of this ignorance is that you take yourself too seriously as an individual. You are worried about your survival, life and death make a great difference. Whether you're alive or dead is extremely important, because when you die as an individual you're finished. There just aren't individuals after death. There are persons, but not individuals. I think this is a very important point because we as Christians do not believe in the afterlife of the individual. We believe in the afterlife of the person, who is free, who is in God already, who is one with God from the beginning. The person returns to God and finds the self in God on a much deeper level than an individual ever could, because an individual has to know the self as an isolated little entity from which everything else is shut off. As long as we're individuals, we can never be one with one another. But, of course, it's as individuals that we work the thing out. So we can talk obliquely about union with God, but there's no answer to the question.

Is it that you try to make a person more conscious?

Conscious of something that's there all the time. But, of course, it is and it isn't. Obviously, when you're aware and conscious of "being" or "I am," then you're a different person, it's a revolution. This is paradoxical. You have to keep qualifying it. But when a person becomes conscious that God is that close, so close that there's no gap, it makes a big difference. Also, when you realize that this presence doesn't depend on being faultless or anything like that, you are different. If it did depend on that, we'd all have to wait a long time for union with God!

Did one of you have a question?

Yes, I have. How do spiritual virginity and spiritual marriage relate to friendship?

This is a part of the same thing. If I regard friendship as a distraction, then it probably is. And if it's a distraction, that means my friend is an object. If the friend is a distraction, the friend is a foreign object in my mind. The answer is not to get rid of friends and to get rid of foreign objects, but to love people in such a way that they're not a foreign object. If you get a foreign object in your eye, it hurts. But if you just get light in your eye, it doesn't hurt at all. We always go back to the central thing. Somebody you love is not a foreign object because you are not foreign to yourself and the person you love is your other self. But we just don't arrive at this by decree. If, in fact, I do love someone else as a foreign object, as a source of satisfaction, I can't say I don't. Usually we talk about a disinterested love, and this is very good. But maybe our love is sentimental and dependent on the other person. When you love someone as an object, what's the consequence? That person has to remain an object in order for you to get the satisfaction you want. You exploit the person. To keep someone as an object is to keep that person in a subservient position, something to be used for your own pleasure. This is a sentimental friendship. The real harm lies in "babying" someone, treating an adult as a minor. When it comes to spiritual virginity, there is such a thing as friendship with other people which is a gift of God. It's not something that can be arrived at just by being smart. It is natural to have mature friendships in which you love the other person because he or she is your other self. It's not distracting at all. You see things in more or less the same way and there's mutual support. A relationship like this can become deeply spiritual because you are, practically speaking, the same person. Therefore, you don't need to rely on it, to be dependent, it doesn't have to be there all the time. I think we've gotten a little more sophisticated on these points, don't you?

Yes, I do. And what you say ties in with the earlier discussion on the rebellion we manufacture in wanting submission. Sometimes a sister does seem to want things difficult and complicated.

Again, we can learn from the Zen people. If somebody wants a complicated answer, give it. Let her worry about it for a while. Pretty soon she'll come back and maybe then can be led to recognize that she didn't need so much complication. If people like this want something intellectual, talk about philosophy or politics. But the way you do it is very important. They will come to you, without realizing it at all, to give you a chance to show how smart you are. You may then feed into this. But if you're conscious, you won't get taken in. You'll lead them, little by little, to see that these things don't matter that much. You'll stay as simple as possible.

As I said before, built into us is a kind of desire for the end, and yet a fear of it, too. We want to attain these things that are beyond us, but we're afraid. As you start getting closer to union with God, it gets tough and we're not really 100 percent for it anyway. So a great deal in us rebels. We've been through the death that's necessary for us to get this far.

Now we want to see if we can't work out some kind of deal so that we can really progress by staying where we are. This is the way we're built as human beings. So we're tempted just to spin all this out in intellectual terms and not really change at all.

But, of course, we're not allowed to do that for long. If we have just enough confidence to let God grab us by the scruff of the neck and drag us through the next thing when we least expect it, then we've got it, we're all right. And we help other people do that as far as we can. I feel very confident about this. None of us is being fooled, we've been through enough to know it's real, that what we are doing is on the level. We are going in the right direction. You'll go home and others will be affected just by the fact that you've been here. It's going to make a big difference.

Now, what are we going to do about this in the future? I think the best thing we can do at the moment is wait. But I think we ought to think in terms of this kind of meeting every once in a while. Father Abbot was saying, "Just once, just once," but he is retiring and I don't think he will influence the future development of things. The prospect for the future looks good. If we can't meet here, we could go to Loretto. So I hope we can plan on something, perhaps with the directors of novices, too. But better to keep the number like this, about fifteen.

Could there be a different program for people working with novices?

There isn't a program. It's just getting together for a visit and sharing. It could be a very good thing if our community and you had much more exchange.

None of the priests in our orders lives a life like you do here.

I know. They're very active and have to preach a lot.

There's no opportunity for sharing with them.

That's right. So it's absolutely essential that, in uncomplicated ways, you share among yourselves. You can get around to each other's places?

It depends on the bishop. But I think you had a great point there about the fact that we might like these barriers.

That's a very deep psychological fact that we're all up against. It's one of the things we have to fight in ourselves, and to learn to cope with, because it's one of the things that will really hold us back. We might keep on doing things in such a way that, instead of attaining the end which we could attain, we're attaining another kind of result. We're creating provocation and resisting and then causing ourselves to be slapped down, so we can just stay where we are and blame it on somebody else.

I think we have to take literally what's said in the motu proprio on religious life, that only the institutes themselves can bring about their own goals. This was sent to us from the Pope himself. So it's a very direct statement.

I have a couple of good biblical texts here on formation. I thought I could read those before we break up. They are useful because our real formation is in the Gospel and in Saint Paul. Saint Paul is forming bishops and Our Lord is forming his apostles. It's wonderful how you can take text after text, and the same text over and over again, and just apply them to different situations, how much light comes out of them in the new situation.

This is Matthew 5:20. "For I tell you, if your virtue goes no deeper than that of the scribes and pharisees, you will never get into the kingdom of heaven." So the first thing is, we must not form scribes and pharisees. "You have learned how it was said to our ancestors, 'You must not kill,' and 'If anyone does kill, he must answer for it before the court.' But I say this to you, 'Anyone who is angry with his brother . . .'" and so on.

What we've been doing, and what I have done with great gusto in the past, is to form scribes and pharisees. That was the system. How easy it was. The new people come to you and you know all the rules, which they don't. You've got an in, a whole esoteric science lined up that you alone know, and here is this helpless, captive audience. They have no clues as to why you hold the cup this way or walk the corridor on that side, but they quickly get the point that this is important in religious life. It's so easy to be an authority under these conditions. Right away it gets to be a tight little system in which everybody knows that the real thing is to know some point of the rule that nobody else knows and to accuse them of it in chapter. Of course, no one does this anymore, but it used to be local sport around here.

I remember my clothing day. In the ceremony, the bishop presents two crowns, one of thorns and one of roses. The novice mistress had kept saying to me, "Now, the bishop's going to say this in Latin. Remember, you answer in English, 'I choose the crown of thorns.'" So when we got to this part, the bishop went into English and I got so frustrated I said, "I'll take the roses!"

Of course! Well, any more questions?

We did touch on this in principle, but I was thinking more about cloister and the world.

I think we agree that there's a hierarchy of things. First, you've got the question of people in active religious life who want to get into more contemplative life. I think any of us, to some extent, should be able to share our life with them. Let them help with the work and take some of the responsibilities. As long as they can live as though they were members of the community, there shouldn't be much problem. They should be bound by the rules. If they want to learn about contemplative life, let them do what the others are doing. That ought to work, and without much distraction. On the other hand, there's the lay person who badly needs a place for retreat. That's different for everyone, it depends on how your community is set up and how well you can manage it. Our guest house here is a waste of time at the moment. Some retreats are canned, and others are preached regularly by

two members of the community. We should be using the
guest house for people who want to come and have silence.
They shouldn't come to be talked *to*, but if they want, they
should have somebody to talk *with*. I think almost everybody in the community should be involved in this in some
way or other. There are all kinds of people in the community, many often kept in the background, who would do very
well in getting together with a guest and taking him around
and showing him things and doing some simple sharing.

How could we do this in our situation? I believe there
should be an overflow from the life of prayer, but it's just
never been a part of our life, even though we often talk to
people through the grille and a lot on the phone.

I think you ought to go out and meet them, sit and talk with
them. If you want to, that is. People who don't want to
should not have to. There should be a choice. If some would
find that distracting or disturbing and want their solitude,
that's fine. But we have to keep in mind that *if* we're going
to share more with people, there's bound to be less silence.
And that will bother some people. Therefore, they should
not have to be in on it. In other words, a much more flexible
setup is needed. Maybe some of those who want more silence won't want it that much all the time. Maybe they will
want to come back and get into these other things. People
could take turns, if they want.

We have sisters who are busy and they come back for the
quiet. One sister is appointed or there's a volunteer who's
available to them if they want to speak with her. But she
never imposes herself, because they are really coming for
the atmosphere.

We had a priest come here from a small town in Texas. He
had a small parish with nobody around much, was about
fifty years old and a quiet type of person. He thought we
would give him a crash course in becoming a contemplative
in two days. So he was completely flabbergasted by the situation I was describing earlier, where you just leave a person

alone. Of course, he realized right away that he had that in Texas. It was perfectly true, so he may as well have stayed where he was. There's no quick course in contemplation. It just doesn't exist. If it does, somebody's being sold a bill of goods.

Sister A: Active sisters today shouldn't be preached at or to, either, but allowed the kind of freedom we've been talking about. There's so much around, all kinds of tapes and books and conferences. What they need, I think, is to be thrown back a little on their own, a chance really to live with themselves in an atmosphere where you can't run away so easily. If people were there to talk and discuss with, that would be good. But not conferences.

Sister B: Do you think there are many among your active sisters who want that?

Sister A: Oh, I think there are very many, Sister, I really do. It would be good to have a list of contemplative houses available where someone could go and be a guest. I was a guest at Mother's abbey and just lived right in with the community. I washed dishes and took my turn at things.

Sister C: And did very well!

Sister A: This is what I appreciated, rather than being off by myself someplace feeling like a guest. I felt like one of the sisters and they shared with me everything they had. It was wonderful. Maybe everybody couldn't do that, but it was a great experience.

Sister D: One of the superiors of a contemplative order just got an answer back from Rome about this. It was NO. They actually talked about the sisters being "contaminated."

What are these people doing? You've got to contribute something. When you really get down to it, it's charity. Charity isn't some big fantastic thing. It's just ordinary love.

And if you love somebody, you invite them in. That's all.

Don't you think we could stop asking for what we don't need to ask for? Some of us have gone on for over seven hundred years, and they don't even know we're living. They don't know a thing about us. They never visit us. They've never had anything to do with us. How about just trying some things?

Sure, that's the sensible thing to do.

The young people are rejecting all this clamping down, it's making them angry. And they have good reason to be.

Exactly. They feel that it's a betrayal. If we get so touchy about falling back on authority, we can't support the young people. We have to have the courage to be on their side. Real charity is involved here. It's a choice between the union of charity with people who are alive and growing and a legalistic union with those who want to hold things back. An individual superior can say to herself at such a point, "I am choosing for Christ when I'm choosing for these people who have real needs and want to experiment and expand."

This is not something I'm just permitted to do, but something I should do. Remember the people who come to you and say, "How do I know which is the better choice?" If you are choosing for life, for a living entity, it's a better choice. If you're choosing for a dead, rigid thing, it's a worse choice. Even if a choice turns out to be imprudent, there's a built-in safeguard because it's *alive*, it's warm, it's real. We have to choose life, always.

PART TWO

Abbey

—— OF ——

Gethsemani

MAY 1968

Contemplative Life as Prophetic Vocation

I want to talk about the prophetic aspect of our vocation. The way I'm going to put it has not been said by anybody. In a certain sense it's a somewhat far-out position, a radical and personal one. In this I'm following a lot of people who are generally outside Church structures and who are very much followed by the young.

All the so-called prophetic movements today are failures because they simply fit into society in another way. The great problem we're up against now is that we live in a society that incorporates dissent into it. In other words, the thesis behind this position is that we're living in a totalitarian society. It's not fascist in a political sense, but in the way that it's economically organized. It's organized for profit and for marketing. In that machinery, there's no real freedom. You're free to choose gimmicks, your brand of TV, your make of new car. But you're not free not to have a car. In other words, life is really determined for everybody. Even the hippies in their dissent are living a predetermined kind of life, although they are trying to get out of it. They rock the boat, there's a splash, everybody is suitably shocked and scandalized, a bit titillated by it. After three years the whole thing vanishes and another fashion starts. It all means nothing.

We as religious fall into that same kind of category. We're good for a certain amount of space in the news, the Vatican Council gets several columns, nuns make some changes. And it's all passé. We're incorporated into a way of life where everything is reduced to a sort of indifference, everything's equal. Page 1 is a nun with a new habit, page 2 is a burlesque queen—equally newsworthy. There's no indication that one

105

thing means more than another. It's just a matter of quantity. Something is worth so much space or so much time on TV. The people I know who are involved in making TV programs say that what's impressive is all the technical expertise that goes into them. What's in front of the camera is indifferent. The important thing is what's happening with the new machinery, not what's going through it. This is the system that calls for some kind of prophetic response.

What are we going to do? What is the prophetic person going to do? The old conservative method of segregation—simply putting people behind grilles—isn't doing anything about this at all. Look back at the history of prophecy, at the Old Testament. One of the essential things about the prophet Abraham is that he's told, "Leave your people." The prophet has to get out of a certain kind of society or social structure. To be a prophet you have to put yourself in the hands of God and go on from there. Moses and the chosen people had to get out of the Egyptian structure. Nothing is said about Egypt being an immoral country. It wasn't necessarily any worse than any other country. But the people had to get out because they weren't free, because somebody else was telling them what to do. Someone else determined their life entirely for them.

The word for this is *alienation,* a word much used by Marx and Freud. Notwithstanding their use of the term, people today are alienated, consciously or unconsciously. Either way, someone else is telling them what they have to do, another is determining how life is to be lived. If people are slaves, it's obvious that somebody else can just decide their lives without any fear of punishment. But in the wage-earning process, too, people's work is generally determined by somebody else's interests; their work has to fit in with another's scheme. But the more people are involved in something set up by others, the less likely they are to be living their own life.

Our society is set up in such a way that people are happy with this. In a police or totalitarian state, you want to get out. Our society gives enough rewards so that you're willing to settle for this, provided you get your car, TV, house, food and drink, and enough other comforts.

A problem arises, of course, when we talk about this, because we're getting into the dangerous area of the old conservative Catholic approach of the world being wicked and that to want material things is bad. It's like turning a crank: the world's no good, give up pleasures, give up money, give up your self-will. The trouble with taking a critical view of the world today is that the average progressive Catholic will immediately say, "That's just the old line."

How can we criticize the world? The world is good. There follows the rather naive approach that says, "Don't give us this business about alienation. We're happy. This is the real life. It's good, it's great." On the other hand, there are people like Lewis Mumford, Jacques Ellul, and Herbert Marcuse, who are saying that the alienated life is not good, that ultimately it's a bad deal because the rewards you get are not real. They are *quantitative*, not qualitative.

In the Old Testament, what happens to Elijah the prophet? He has to stand completely alone against the whole structure. At one point, he's got Jezebel and all the army after him and he has to flee. He goes into the desert, he's off to Mount Sinai, he hides in a cave. He's starving, and ravens bring him food. Here we're at the heart of the prophetic, Carmelite tradition. Something similar happens to Saint Francis. For him, too, there's a radical break with the world into a prophetic and free life where he made his own choices. This is the essential thing. John the Baptist is another example. Whenever you make a choice from your own deepest center, you are not being predetermined by somebody else.

One of the central issues in the prophetic life is that a person rocks the boat, not by telling slaves to be free, but by telling people who *think* they're free that they're slaves. That's an unacceptable message. There's nothing new about telling the blacks that they're having a rough time. The prophetic thing in this country is to tell white people that they need the blacks to be free *so they'll be liberated themselves*. Few people say this. James Baldwin does. Many people think that some whites are trying to give the blacks something and that the blacks are doing the whites a favor by accepting it. And that this is going to make everything just fine. We've got to realize that this kind of "progressive" position can be as much of a trap as anything else.

If we're going to live up to our prophetic vocation, we have to realize that, whether we're revolutionary or not, we have to be radical enough to dissent from what is basically a totalitarian society. And we're in it. It's not a society that's coming, it is here. So we really do need to pay attention to some of the people we mentioned earlier, even though they are sometimes regarded as pessimists. We also need to pay attention to the prophets in Scripture who are called away from their people to stand on a different ground where they can choose freely before God, where they can make choices not predetermined by society.

We have to face the fact that the contemplative life as set up today is not only non-prophetic; it's anti-prophetic. It's designed to block any kind of prophetic reaction at all. If someone did something prophetic around here, it would upset the whole place, the community would be shocked. We'd have no way of handling it. We're trying to arrive at a systematic adjustment where everybody has a great deal of free time, a minimum of work, with nobody on his back. This is nice, but it's not the contemplative life.

I think we can settle for something better. Not just individuals but the community itself should be prophetic. That's an ideal, of course. But that's our task: not to produce prophetic individuals who could simply end up as a headache, but to be a prophetic community.

Then we don't try to identify with the people of our time?

We do and we don't. We have to be to them a sign of contradiction which reminds them of a freedom they've forfeited. But that means we ourselves have to have that freedom or be struggling for it, if we don't. I think we can learn from the ones in the world who know something about this. Ping Ferry is someone who's very much in touch with the secular prophetic element in this country, both black and white. The black community as a whole tends to be prophetic. Some of the black, far-out jazz, for example, is really protest music. It's almost incomprehensible, but if you listen to it, you find there's a great deal of depth to it. Some of it is very disconcerting, frightful noises made with reeds. Soul music is an expression of anger and hurt and even more. It's completely different from the innocuous Muzak, accepted by white society, that you hear in the dentist's office, totally the opposite.

In our official religious lives, there are structures which block awareness and which substitute gestures as a kind of symbolic front or image. They're like a prescription or recipe you write out: Get up at two o'clock in the morning, never write home, never eat meat, never miss choir. You make the list and then do it. You could be standing asleep in choir, it's okay. We said we were going to do it and we did! This is what we're up against. Doing these things gives a feeling of security, something we can feel and see and touch, a new materialism. It's reassuring. Take the structure away and some people may not recognize themselves. What does this mean? It means that we can be completely alienated people, that our identity is immersed in a structure which has been devised for and by somebody else. When we're in that structure we feel at peace; when we're out of it, we don't exist.

So before we can become prophetic, we have to be authentic human beings, people who can exist outside a structure, who can create their own existence, who have within themselves the resources for affirming their identity and their freedom in any situation in which they find themselves. This means people capable of creating a life for themselves who are not identified with a structure.

Unfortunately, it's possible to change and yet do the same thing in a different context. Everyone can see how silly it is to go to choir at 2:00 a.m., when you're on your last legs, but may not see that drinking whiskey with somebody at 2:00

a.m. is the same conformity turned inside out, another way of doing what's approved or accepted. It's just a new line, another structure.

We're being encouraged to identify ourselves with a secular culture that in its own way offers a kind of security and comfort, but which, in fact, swallows up our liberty because it's a totalitarian structure. This is the problem Marcuse and people like him are talking about.

People who get caught up in this progressive thing can become very cynical.

It's possible. Even though there's a certain freedom in our society, it's largely illusory. Again, it's the freedom to choose your product, but not the freedom to do without it. You have to be a consumer and your identity is to a large extent determined by your choices, which are very much determined by advertising. Identity is created by ads. You choose your brand of Scotch because you identify with the image conveyed by that brand. It's very instructive to read the ads. We should be able to do that critically; people who are dominated by them don't so much read them as react to them in a kind of instinctive way, their consciousness only half on. You can read them because you don't take them seriously. I may like the Peck and Peck ads because what I'm telling myself is that they represent the kind of girl I would like to have married.

Real smart and likes the right things!

That's the pitch. And that's where they get the non-conforming people!

Do you see non-conformity as basic to the monastic vocation, that this is typical of true contemplatives?

Oh, yes.

I think psychologists have found that out from testing adjusted contemplatives.

Sure. The desert life was a life of non-conformity, it was a protest. It's a cliché to say that now, but Protestants like Harnack were the ones who said it. The desert people were protesting against the union of Church and empire under Constantine. When the Church became a respectable establishment, people started going into the desert. They talked about it in terms of there being no more martyrdom, so they had to suffer in some other way. But they simply wanted to get out because they thought that things weren't authentic anymore. They were certainly trying to get away from bishops, although the propaganda never admitted it. Athanasius got involved with the monks and they were dragged into the structure to help fight off the Arians. So they were back in the establishment. The Egyptian monks were very much into politics and, with Origen, the picture got really bad.

But the Syrian monks stayed out of this, as did many groups who had little to do with the rest of the Church. Of course, historians play that *down*. The whole picture has really been turned inside out. Monks were the great supporters of orthodoxy. What we have to look out for is the fact of living in a trapped society.

This society blocks *qualitative* change while it foments *quantitative* change. New products, new gimmicks are everywhere. We can buy more and different things and replace them quickly because they get obsolete so fast. The human race has never been so standardized and so bound to a predetermined situation as it is today.

We talk about the Middle Ages as if they were ages of unfreedom. But if you read a little more history you find out how much people could really choose for themselves. True, the philosophy of life was predetermined. But there was a lot you could do. People like Saint Bernard, for example, were very independent and roamed about freely. Sometimes you get the feeling that people then were tied down to one place, but actually they were very mobile.

Today's society also allows for change, but it neutralizes protest and can absorb a lot of it. So peace efforts, no matter how much they rock the boat, aren't going to change anything. People are beginning to see that and are getting desperate, because it's a terrible situation. If you're aware of this, you see how helpless we are. As for us, we're in a double bind, because not only are we resisting a conservative structure of our own but, even if we get out of it, we're still in something that isn't really that free. We need to find out just to what extent we can live our own lives.

But that can easily become a privileged situation. Take solitude, for example. I'm probably living my own life as much as anybody in the country. But solitude's a luxury. Only a few millionaires have solitude—and a few bums. Of course, bums aren't just that; many of them choose it. It's a drastic choice, but some persons want the freedom it gives. Not that they aren't trapped, too, but they do have a certain mobility. But they have to pay a price: it's a dirty and insecure and depressing life. Think what it would be like to live at the bottom of the pile all the time. People like Benedict Joseph Labré chose that sort of life. It has a monastic character because it's a separation, a way of saying, "I don't *have* to be a respectable person. I don't have to accept the values that everybody says I do."

Built into society are certain dictates. You have to do this or you have to do that. If you do these things, you're happy. If you don't, you're unhappy, you're a failure, you're bad, you're rejected. Never before now has that been so systematized. The bums say, "If you do this, do that, you're *not* happy. You just say you are. I'm going to do something else which doesn't have these things. And I'm going to be happy."

That's what we're doing. There's something in us that never gives us any peace unless we're doing that. But the Church structure comes along and says, "If you do this, you'll be happy, you'll be pleasing to God, you'll be a good religious, you'll be a saint." And something in us says, "That's not true. In order to be happy and to be a saint, I have to follow my conscience, I have to follow the Holy Spirit." This is the root of our prophetic vocation. We have to see it in this light. Nobody's going to tell us what to do except God and our conscience and our brothers and sisters. No one is going to determine our lives.

But symbolic protest isn't enough. We've really got to live. And this may be a much less spectacular thing than protesting. Nobody may notice our lives. But we know what we are doing.

Each of us must measure up to our own vocation, we must be ourselves. We may not have to measure up to the program of any monastery or order, but we do have to live our own lives. If we don't do this, we're of no use to anyone. The purpose of today's talk is to realize that no one else can live our lives for us. There's no conservative or progressive program, no paper or magazine, no NCR or *Osservatore Romano* that can tell us what to do and how to live.

In a certain sense, we know what we need to do. Much of it is doing what we realistically want. We don't just follow our fantasies, we're willing to fight for our right to do what we want. We don't come to this decision alone; we check it out with other people. We help one another do this. We all live in a community, so the community has to be involved. A meeting like this, without going into a revision of life, supports us. So what we want to do is more than just a personal thing.

The question is, then: What do you want to do in your communities? Adjust that to what is reasonably possible and do it. We won't then be led astray by fallacious promises from somebody else. See what you can do with what you've got and with what's open to you. A lot of things can happen after that. My own problem is to see how I can help you without getting involved in a great lecture circuit or something of that kind.

So let us pray together: In the name of the Father and the Son and the Holy Spirit. Amen. O Lord, grant us your light and the strength of your Holy Spirit to follow our vocation as you would wish us to; and grant us the grace to understand the problems of that vocation in the light of your will for our time. Through Christ our Lord.
Amen.

Prophecy, Alienation, Language

Yesterday we talked about the prophetic aspect of our vocation. I wanted to get down to the most fundamental root of our life—the prophetic function. I was saying that this is not accounted for, either by the conservative approach or by the progressive approach. The conservative approach wants to fit us into a medieval society; the progressive, into modern society. Neither of these is prophetic. So we're caught between two traps. This is hardly ever talked about.

The conservative viewpoint says: Hold on to the tradition of the founders and the structures that have come down so far; they're adequate, they work. For us, this view has a certain value, for we know that buried in it somewhere is the prophetic character of our vocation. All we have to do is recover it. The progressive view says: Get with the modern world because it's prophetic. Join the liberal, radical advance in society because revolution is prophetic or social change within the structure is prophetic.

The standpoint I take is from the point of view of some modern thinkers, like Herbert Marcuse, who are very influential among the young today. Marcuse is not Catholic, but he's a kind of monastic thinker. His idea of freedom is the kind that we're constituted for. Like the young, he is radically questioning structures. Most of the newer generation are not Marxists at all, but neither do they fit into present cultural patterns. They get a bit anarchistic and wild sometimes, but this has to be understood. The revolution of the French students now is very significant: it expresses the frustration of people who have nowhere to go, so all they can do is explode. Not that this helps. It's no solution. But it has to be expected.

The question for us is: Are we going to be caught in a

114

society that is much more permissive than the rigid ones of Marxism but yet also totalitarian? This is never admitted, but it's true in the sense that everything important is really determined for people beforehand. What's left is trivial. You cannot make choices that really influence the society itself.

An example occurs to me here, the Poor People's March on Washington. Everyone knows in advance that nothing's going to change. This is reflected in the thinking of the people who go when they say, "This is your last chance. If nothing happens now, you're going to have a lot of trouble." They foresee there'll be no real change. A report from someone in Washington quotes a black woman from the ghetto who tried to communicate with an official there. "I'm going to tell you the kind of life that me and my husband live. Our ceiling fell in and he was hurt and needs crutches. . . ." Then her husband breaks in and tries to describe how things are. Finally the woman says, "And if you people don't do something, we're going to do like Jesus. We're going to come back again." The officials just listened, smiled, and said, "Thank you for coming." Something like the response to Saint Paul at the Acropolis: "Glad to have you here to express your opinion. We'll think about it sometime." A brush-off.

It's like trying to fight without having someone oppose you.

Sure. It is something for people to get a chance to express themselves. In other societies they couldn't. Better at least to be able to speak. But it's also very frustrating when you know that speaking out doesn't mean anything to the ones you're speaking to. This is what I was bringing out yesterday. With all the protest groups, there is the growing realization that protest really doesn't change anything. We would like to stop the Vietnam War, but our country is committed to a position that makes that impossible. Our system is set up in such a way that, if the war stopped, everybody would be in a turmoil. The war has to continue because everything is built around it.

Take the race issue. The reason nothing can be done is that we really don't want to do anything. Whites want the advantage of being kind to blacks, but they don't want blacks living next door. They foresee that it's going to be tough for their children, bad for the school, and for property values. So although white people in theory want the good things for everybody, it can't be done in practice.

That's the real point. If you can't actually do something, you're not free. Something prevents your making the big decisions. They're predetermined. That's what we're up against with issues like the Vietnam War and civil rights. Things can't be changed because the price is too high: a total upheaval of society. Nobody's willing to do this. Maybe eventually it will happen, we don't know. This is the situation we're in.

Why do I say all this to contemplatives? Some might say, "Well, we've left all that, it means nothing to us. We're with God and we pray for all these people. We're sorry it's this way, but we're dead to it."

The only answer to that is, We're not dead. We're part and parcel of this world. Who buys Trappist cheese? We eat three times a day. This fact puts us firmly in the context of a society where people are working and making money and where a certain system of production is going on. We're part of it. Either that or don't eat! What can a Carmel do in the middle of Roxbury? Symbolic actions, mostly. But you can express goodwill. In some way or other, you can let these people know, "We're with you."

Now I want to get back to the basic problem of living in an alienated society. The basic reason for a monastic or contemplative life is the realization that, in following the ordinary approved paths, you cannot live your own life. This has to be taken into account when we consider the genuineness of a vocation. How deep is this realization in the young people coming to join us? To what extent are they running away from the risks of a life which is disturbing to them, and just looking for a tranquil backwater where they will not be disturbed? This is a matter of immense importance for us because for centuries the religious life in European civilization has been a quiet backwater where people who can't negotiate the problems of society have a refuge. This has been exploited for hundreds of years by rich European families: the royal but unmarriageable daughter was put in a convent. There existed many aristocratic convents in France and other countries for wealthy princesses who were put on the shelf because they couldn't marry in a way that pleased the family. Of course, all convents weren't like that, but it was a widespread problem.

Let me say more about living in a predetermined society. The prophetic vocation to which we are called as religious involves a deep awareness of the contradictions in society. We have to feel this keenly. Otherwise, our vocation is going to be watered down or we're going to miss its point. Being called out of the world is not a matter of skipping movies because they're no good or giving up dancing because it's frivolous.

We're called to religious life because otherwise we're not free to act from our deepest center, to follow the deepest needs of our life. A person who is aware of that and is hurting on account of that has a genuine vocation. That's why we exist. We're supposed to provide a place where people can find something that they cannot find elsewhere. This seems to be getting lost or obscured because the progressive line about religion tends more and more to identify reality and authenticity purely and simply with what's going on in secular society.

This is precisely one of the characteristics of modern society that Marcuse analyzes. He calls his book *One-Dimensional Man*, and he's talking about life in an advanced, industrial society that has one dimension. By this he means a society where everything is reduced to the lowest common denominator and everybody fits into that. Things are organized so that you can fit in easily and even happily. The person who fits in painlessly, who reads *Time* and *Life*, who does all the approved things, watches all the approved programs, answers the Gallup poll, and is content doing these things is "one-dimensional." When everybody fits into this mold, then everything will work smoothly, everyone will make lots of money, the products will go round, the Gross National Product will go up, everybody will pay their taxes, blacks will keep their mouths shut, and we will win all our wars.

As a liberal, you might say there are a few things wrong with this picture but these can be changed. Or you might be more revolutionary and say the whole thing is wrong. So you blow it all up and put it together again exactly as it was before but with different people running it. People who are progressive about the problems of religious life now tend to say that what's needed is for us to get out of the Middle Ages and become one-dimensional modern people.

This is the source of untold trouble for us. First of all, most contemplatives don't want to move at all. They are afraid to move because they're not being offered a valid alternative and because they are not properly informed. But their sense is right. What we had in the past may have been unsatisfactory, but at least we know what it was. Better to keep that than lose everything. They fear being robbed of their identity by some unknown happening.

This situation is complicated by the fact that most contemplatives, I would say, are deeply afflicted by a certain sense of guilt; they realize they have not been very contemplative at all. Many have been missing the point, sidestepping the whole thing. We've been elevating the contemplative mystique, we have a few formulas about it which we revere. But, in fact, we haven't been freed up to develop interiorly. We've even lost the concept that this is something we ought to do. We have provided a solid and predictable structure that had some validity, but a lot of it was useless. It was easy to teach novices. You had all the inside information on a lot of rules that nobody could possibly guess existed. But you knew. And you trained new people to keep these rules. It kept you busy and it kept them busy. Everybody got the impression that something was really going on.

But, in point of fact, it was left to individuals, if they wanted, to make something out of their lives. And with a lot of work and a lot of fidelity, they did. This would work nicely for five or ten years. Then they became superiors and got into the same bind as everybody else. They had to organize, there were problems, they had to make the best of it. A certain amount of reality comes in here, nothing's perfect, and some things have worked out okay. But for a large number of people in contemplative orders, there's been a sense of unease, a kind of malaise, a feeling that if you wanted something deeper, you were prevented from getting it. There were probably many reasons for this, one being the fear that maybe it was all too risky and even dangerous.

Take the question of the hermit life. Not long ago, it was totally disapproved. The standard answer: It's impossible, it's a delusion, it can't be right. People accepted that. Yet there was a nagging sense that maybe you really ought to do it. You couldn't quite shake loose from the idea. Then it occurred to somebody: Let those who want, try it. Nobody had ever thought of that before. There's been a tremendous improvement now; people have more leeway to experiment. If you try something and it doesn't work, you'll know in your heart it was a bum steer, and then you're free of it.

One of the things that people do *not* want is to be one-dimensional, they don't want to be forced into a mold. It's important that we not be taken in by a superficial idea of freedom which says that liberty consists in getting in with one-dimensional society and doing the things it approves. Let me quote Marcuse: "Most of the prevailing needs to relax, to have fun, to behave and consume in accordance with the advertisements, to love and hate what others love and hate, belong to the category of false needs." Marcuse is making the point that what makes us conform to this kind of society is not at all a question of a Hitler-like dictatorship, which we don't have, but a question of needs. Our society makes people need things and need them so badly that everything is put aside for the sake of fulfilling these needs. Mostly these are needs for certain types of consumer goods. The reason we can't stop the war, end the problems of the poor, and eliminate the race problem is that we are so bound by the needs created by our economy that we have no choice. The alternative is unacceptable. To change, we would have to do without a lot of things and live a totally different style of life. We would not have the same kind of secure feeling.

Religious people have to be aware of these false needs. This is actually not a new but a very traditional idea. It's important not only to recognize false needs but also to see why they are false. We used to be told a lot about the vanity of the world and its hypocrisy, but this was a kind of party line. Actually, having accepted all of this, we got into another little system that was just like the first, only it offered a different kind of comfort and a different kind of security.

Another point that Marcuse is very good on is the whole question of language. What's happening in language today? It's an important area of exploration. He talks about how the German language was altered during the Nazi period to distort the truth, how it was systematically used to say that things are what they aren't, to make them appear black when they're white. He shows how disastrous this was in its effects.

Language today is going through changes, too. When we are exposed, without a discerning faculty, to just the ordinary talk that goes on, to what comes over the mass media, we lose our ability to have any kind of accurate perspective on what's happening. We lose touch with reality. It's the old question of "Should nuns read *Time?*" Well, yes and no. If the question means, should nuns be informed? the answer is, definitely. But if it implies that by reading *Time* you are informed, then no.

What makes this clear is that all the sources of information have a kind of lingo about them which presupposes a whole new attitude toward reality; namely, that if you let yourself be hypnotized by what's said, you get in touch with reality. You think you are informed, but you're living in an imaginary world, which is nevertheless accepted by all the people who think the same way. Marcuse talks about language being compressed into little capsules so that it cuts down on any length or development of thought. You get the facts through the impact of these small packets thrown at you. The rest is by implication. In other words, you don't actually think about what's said. You construct a series of images which make you react in a sort of global and imaginative way. This leads to what Marcuse calls "arrested development in self-validating hypnotic formulas." A self-validating formula is a statement that's incontrovertible because it's a tautology. It's absurd. The model of this is the statement of the officer in Vietnam who said they had to destroy a certain town in order to save it. This is the way the abuse of language functions.

Statements like that are being made all the time, just maybe not quite as crass. In an essay that I wrote on war and language, I've got a few examples of that. One is an ad for perfume. There's a picture of a glamorous model in a kind of ecstasy because she has this perfume. The ad reads, "There's a new hair spray. The world's most adored fragrance now in a hair spray. But not a hair spray as you know it. A delicate hair spray. Your hair takes on a shimmer and sheen that's wonderfully young. You seem to spray new life and bounce right into it. And a coif of Arpège has one more thing that no other hair spray has. It has Arpège." In spite of the fact that anybody who reflects on this ad can see that it's stupid, it's also hypnotic. The reason it's hypnotic is that it's narcissistic, which is what a closed circle always is. The poor girl who reads the ad gets a good feeling of herself being adorable because she uses this hair spray. She gets a sense of identity and a sense of worth and the whole thing is utterly false. She's been *had*.

We say "she" but this happens to all of us. To get me, it has to be something slightly more sophisticated. For instance, if you say, "Sartre just said this about existentialism," then I'll have to follow it up! Here is the latest thinking on a topic, here is a breakthrough in existentialist thought. It's the same thing all down the line, the same mechanism. You are presented the image of a seductive product and you allow yourself to be seduced by it and then feel better. You're happy.

Political statements are made in this particular kind of way. Candidate X gets up and gives you one of these packages. You come away feeling better. Maybe I'll vote for this candidate. The same kind of presentation as in the ads. The image counts. How do you feel about the whole world situation in terms of this image? If the person's attractive and says nice things, people respond in terms of how they feel. It's really a commercial. None of it is politically relevant, even though it may try to be.

These are examples of self-validating, hypnotic formulas which are immune to contradictions. You can't contradict the fact that Arpège has Arpège. But the point is: does it matter? Who cares? You don't ask that kind of question. This is a subtle insight—people actually don't care. If they did care, they'd fight. Not really caring much about anything profound is characteristic of one-dimensional people. It might as well be Arpège. Why not? It gets back to feeling free because I can buy my own brand of soap. But fundamentally, I don't care.

I once caused consternation in a drugstore in Louisville. I was going to the hospital and I wanted to get some toothpaste, so I went in and said, "I'd like some toothpaste." The clerk says, "What kind?" and I said, "I don't care." He almost dropped dead. I was supposed to feel strongly about Colgate or Pepsodent or Crest or something with five colors. And they all have a secret ingredient. But I didn't care about the secret ingredient. The worst thing you can do now is not care about these things.

The abuse of language really blocks thinking and is a substitute for it. "It repels recognition of the factors behind the facts." Now, an essential thing about a prophetic vocation is awareness of factors behind the facts. One-dimensional society doesn't want this. Factors behind facts complicate life too much, they could create problems. We'd have to stop and tussle with things and make some changes.

When we leave out the historical content of facts, the result is a loss of historical consciousness. We are no longer the kind of historical beings that previous generations were.

History is being lost to us. This can be seen in the problem of religious renewal. A European friend remarked that renewal in America is very different, because we have no tradition that goes farther back than the nineteenth century. And our nineteenth-century background is not very satisfactory, either. But once you throw that out, you've thrown out everything. This is disturbing to the conservatives who feel that at least there was a past they could look back to with some satisfaction. Now we're starting over again from scratch. That's not necessary, but it's part of the American myth. America renounced Europe when the Puritans came over. That was the end of history as far as they were concerned. We were starting a whole new life, a new creation, the kingdom.

But we don't have to be that way. It's instructive to have a history, because mistakes have been made before that we don't need to make again. For better or worse, the young people have thrown everything out and feel they have to start all over again. They've got to make the mistakes that have been made for centuries, all by themselves. It's going to be rough, but it's their choice.

Talking and feeling in these terms helps people conform more or less painlessly. This is the condition on which one-dimensional society depends. We are trained to tune in to messages of this kind and that keeps everything going. George Orwell did a good job on this in 1984. Also, *Animal Farm* was about a completely one-dimensional society. That's the kind of society we're in now.

To live prophetically, you've got to be questioning and looking at factors behind the facts. You've got to be aware that there are contradictions. In a certain sense, our prophetic vocation consists in hurting from the contradictions in society. This is a real cross in our lives today. For we ourselves are partly responsible. An even greater cross for many of us are the contradictions in the Church. And the contradictions in our own background and in our own Christian lives, contradictions for which we are not totally responsible but which we have to live with and face constantly. We have to work with them and resist the temptation to scapegoat others. Read the prophets in the Old Testament. Their biggest problem was that they were prophets. Jeremiah didn't want to be a prophet. In some sense, we're in the same boat. God lays on us the burden of feeling the contradictions in our world and Church and exposing them, insofar as we are honestly able to do that.

What does a contemplative do about this? The mere fact of living in silence, a kind of silence that might be called electric with this sense of contradiction, is important. Our silence can't be just nice and cozy, narcissistic and sweet. It's a silence in which there is pain, where we know we *should* say something but haven't got anything to say. People should be able to sense that our silence comes from deep reflection and honest suffering about the contradictions in the world and in ourselves. Instead, they often see us living a silence that is reassuring and pleasing to our benefactors, in which the world's all right, after all.

Well, we should be happy and smiling. But that's not all. If we take seriously the importance of language, we see that the way it's used now, there's no gap between naming a thing and pronouncing a judgment about it; judgment is more or less built into the naming. For example, if I say the word *freedom,* it means freedom only in a certain context, that of free enterprise. Freedom used in any other context is not freedom. Everything is packed into a confined definition. All I have to do is say "freedom," nothing else. You don't say "Freedom is good" or "Freedom is what we've got." It's a *closed* language; it does not demonstrate and explain. It communicates decision already built in. If you don't agree with this idea of freedom, you're going to have some explaining to do. That's what we're up against.

The Feminine Mystique

The topic I'd like to talk about this afternoon is the "feminine mystique." I think it's a real problem, which all of you already realize. Of course, I'm no authority on this; I'll just start us thinking and maybe you can do the talking. Underlying this feminine mystique is the fact that women take an awful beating and have a very tough time in the Church. So they tend to buy into this mystique and cooperate with it.

What is this feminine mystique? It's an idealization of supposed special feminine qualities which are put up on a pedestal and made much of. It's also tied in with a cloistered, contemplative mystique. The woman is said to be essentially such and such, like "passive" and "mysterious." But *everybody* is mysterious and sometimes passive. These things are not specialties of women. To make a mystique out of things like this is nonsense. But many people, including some women, like it.

It's part of the game that's been going on between men and women for centuries. I think women have seen through it long before men, but many elected to go along with it. There's some notion that women have a particular kind of intuitive wisdom, which is true to a great extent. But you don't deify it. Men are also intuitive. Or there's the idea that women are not rational the way men are. But they *are*. All this sounds as if women and men are two specifically different kinds of beings, as if each had a different nature.

This resembles what we find in the race question: stereotypes about the blacks as if they were essentially different in being, like "more compulsive" or "more passionate." These things are just not true. But if you elevate them to the level of dogma and say they are true, you *make* them true.

This is the way language functions in our society. If you say something long enough, everybody begins to believe it.

We have to face the fact that the cloistered contemplative nun has been "officially" appointed to live out this feminine mystique. I think you have an absolute duty to rebel, for the good of the Church itself. Otherwise, you are creating and perpetuating this image of the mysterious, veiled, hidden woman who is an "enclosed garden." The truth is not that there's all this "femininity" locked up in a convent. The truth is that there are *people* loving God. But this truth gets obscured in a mystique. People miss the whole point.

It's time to end this mystique, which does no one any good. As Mary Daly brings out so clearly in her book, what happens is that, in one and the same breath, women are idealized and humiliated by it. This mystique is an instrument of oppression for women. All the trouble you're having with the bishops and with Rome occurs in the name of this mystique. If you're going to liberate yourselves, you have to break out of this image, this view that you can't make your own decisions because you're passive and mysterious and veiled and different. What this has to do with men's psychology is an enormous story. You know that this whole question of the relation between the sexes has a long history. As I understand it, in the Neolithic period women really ran things, society was largely matriarchal. There was a long period of a more or less dominant feminine culture, a period of several thousand years. There's no history for this period because there didn't need to be; it was a peaceful village society. This pre-history time had strong feminine values, but of course, you can't push that too far, because you'll get the same mystique in reverse. Nevertheless, the time was less warlike and society had more balance.

When we get into the city culture, about 1000–500 B.C., there's a cultural shift into a war-making society, and the establishment of a hierarchical, priestly society with men at the top. When the society was run by women, it was not hierarchical but, rather, wide open, with a certain amount of respect for feminine values, insofar as they exist. With structures built by men, society became more warlike and businesslike. Women got pushed into a "special role" in society. A woman then became a commodity and was dealt with more and more as a "thing."

This treatment of women can happen with or without a feminine mystique. But the mystique developed to help the situation be more acceptable to women and to men. By the end of the Roman culture, this treatment of women had reached the end of its limits. So the beginning of religious life for women was a real liberation. You can tell this from the letters that Jerome wrote to women who were making vows as virgins or who were entering embryonic religious communities. They show women leaving behind the married life then available, a life in which they were simply a possession of a rather uncouth and brutal husband. Religious life was an opportunity for women to have a certain liberty of being, a chance to be a *person*. And it was about the only place this was possible. Jerome, for all his faults, had the sense not only to see this but also to promote it.

Simone de Beauvoir, who is quoted by Mary Daly, also comes up against this fact of the religious life and of Christian women mystics. She struggles with it and repudiates a lot of it, saying it is sick. But she admits to being greatly impressed by Saint Teresa: "This woman really had it!" So, although Simone de Beauvoir thinks that religious life was a way of keeping women down, she sees that there were those who broke through. This was especially true of the medieval abbesses. Beauvoir makes a certain point of the fact that for a long time there were quite a few double communities in monasticism in which the abbess ran a community of women and of men. They were separate, of course, but it was a workable solution and, to some extent, a kind of re-establishment of women. In these places, women directed men and this was more or less accepted and understood.

Simone de Beauvoir also sees the friendship of Teresa and John of the Cross as a very good thing. It was fine because here were two *real people*. This is very interesting because it's the same thing with the French Marxist Garaudy, whose specialty is being in dialogue with Catholics. He doesn't go along with much of Catholicism, but he comes out with things like "The one thing that Catholics have that we Marxists don't is somebody like Saint Teresa," and he wonders if and how that can be explained.

You can't use Teresa too well as an example of the feminine mystique. Why? Because she's a real, whole person. To build a feminine mystique you have to cut somebody in half. The same is true of a masculine mystique. In this country we're up against a great problem with both aspects of this situation.

The American man is half a human being, with his masculinity overemphasized. Think of the things a man cannot allow himself to do because he thinks they're feminine. He's not allowed to have kind or tender feelings. He has to avoid being fastidious about cleanliness. A man is not supposed to be very concerned about the lives of animals or trees; this is considered sentimental. A tree is worth so many dollars, cut it down and sell it. And animals exist for hunting. To be a man you have to be somewhat destructive and insensitive, not open to feelings, because they're for women.

Women in this country, for their part, suffer from a double mystique. In addition to the pedestal mystique, there's what might be called the Playboy mystique. It's no good at all and reflects very badly on American men. Most of you don't see Playboy and neither do I. But it might be an education to look at it sometime. I know people who have the magazine around their homes. They're not totally uncritical, but they accept it as fairly normal, something to be taken for granted. *Taken for granted!* If you know a little about psychoanalysis you will know that this is not to be taken for granted at all. It's extremely sick.

I think that behind this Playboy attitude toward women is a fear of women. This attitude presupposes that if women are admitted to be in any way equal to men, and not just a toy of some sort, then men have to be wary, they are threatened, they fear not being able to survive the competition. This is an indication of a very sick situation. I'm no pro in this field and I haven't studied it, but it's really worth examining because it has far-reaching effects on everybody, on our whole society.

Inevitably, this attitude of sexual competitiveness is going to have effects on the religious life, and on priests. A priest tends to shy away from all that, but if he assumes that this is the normal male attitude toward women, then he's going to be reinforced in his idea that women can't be trusted. And, of course, this is the problem with a lot of priests. So many of them have no notion whatever of how to relate to a woman, that she is simply another person, a human being, and not a natural cataclysm of some sort. Behind the whole situation is the exploitation of women.

Now the cloistered nun enters the picture. All your struggles for freedom, for the things you want to do, run up against this obstacle, that is, against men who in one way or another think about women in these two ways at the same time. On the one hand, they've got a contemplative mystique; on the other, they've got some unsavory notions of women as depicted in Playboy.

I think this is a real part of our problem. The men in Rome project onto us what they see or feel or imagine.

Certainly it is a problem. We see again how the whole history of marriage in Europe as a kind of business deal, with no real love involved, enters in here. In European situations, it's often taken for granted that a man's sexual fulfillment is not in the home but elsewhere. This is also an accepted standard in Latin American culture. It is a bad and unhealthy situation, it's sick.

Every time I've talked about religious life to the cardinal in Rome, I know even before I start that he isn't going to hear anything I say. Because right away he says, "Yes, yes, yes"; in other words, "Finish as fast as you can, because first, you're a woman, and second, you're an

American." No matter what reasons I put before him, or whatever I really say, it doesn't mean a thing.
You're beaten from the start. That's the European kind of mentality I was talking about. There are deep implications for everybody in the way of thinking and the problems we've opened up here. They are present in family life. For example, in how many families is there an unspoken battle going on between the father and the mother simply because they're different sexes? They themselves don't understand or know this. How many brothers and sisters are unconsciously brought up in such a way that they're afraid of each other or suspicious of each other? There's some kind of tension between them. This overemphasis on sexual differences is a tremendous problem in the world of our time.

We need to understand this problem. It's part of your task at present to break it wide open. This will require a whole different relationship with people outside the cloister. If you maintain the mystique in which you are forced to live now, you will perpetuate the problem. Of course, you have to live your life, you can't just rebel. Being more open with people, dealing with them as persons, being just who you are already strikes people favorably when they come in contact with you. They often say, "Well, they're real people." That shows exactly where the answer lies.

Cloister discipline does, to some extent, contribute to a person's development. So we can't just throw the whole thing out. But it may contribute less than we think. It may be only the relic of an old culture. Every culture has some validity, and medieval culture was great, but it's past. It's based on an idealization which enables society to use women for its own interests, ultimately. And that's alienation.

If I am living in such a way that it is really more for somebody else's interests than for my own good, I am living an alienated life. You, as cloistered nuns, are to some extent having to live a life that is not for you, but for someone else's advantage; in other words, for the advantage of a social structure and an institutional structure. You are to some extent justified. And people in Rome want you to continue to be as you are. But it's an alienating situation and you have to rectify it. It has to be changed.

Unfortunately, some very intelligent people don't see this. Here is a quote from Teilhard de Chardin, who is ordinarily quite smart: "Woman is a luminous and inspiring influence outside the throes of tumult and action." But if you're outside the throes of tumult and action, you're not participating in life. This gets us back to the idea that a woman's task is to do the dishes, that her place is strictly in the home. (Of course, when we get up to my hermitage, you certainly will see in less than five seconds that a woman's touch is missing. Just wanted to make that clear before you got there!)

Another part of the mystique is the glorification of the mother. A man can get so narcissistic, wanting to have Mom around to comfort him. This reveals a guilty, sick, and ambivalent attitude toward women on the part of men. Men stand to gain by the rehabilitation of women; men will be more whole when women are. What everybody has to be is a *person*. Wholeness is in the reciprocity between men and women as persons who have the same nature. Differences are there and these need to be taken into account, but differences are not decisive. The same thing applies to race. It's not decisive whether a person is white or black. It makes some difference but not an essential one. The same is true for a Frenchman or an American: the difference is there, but it's not decisive. It's wrong to judge persons on the basis of these differences.

Then, of course, there's the male reaction of misogyny. Many men and a lot of clerics are really women-haters. They're afraid of women and they deal with women as if they were enemies, in a tricky or dishonest way. We've all met men who will not talk straight to a woman and who always have a special routine for women. They'll talk straight to another man, but for women they've got a lot of flimflam, or they beat around the bush. Women, of course, can do the same thing to men. It all adds up to the fact that women have a secondary place. This is what's wrong, plain wrong: men on top and women in second place.

As long as things are like that, there can't be any significant reform in the religious life. Women have to be able to run things; certainly they have to have their part in running their own lives. This is fundamentally essential if there's going to be any further change. You need to have a say, and that will not be easy. Men have to be educated on this point.

This bias shows up in civil government, and it's worse in religion.

It's very entrenched in religion, where men have the advantage of having held things back to the medieval level. At least in the government and in business, things have moved forward. In the religious environment you just get a talk on "The Metaphysical World of Women." Imagine!

"The psychology of woman" kind of response.

Exactly. You can get sick of all this. It's not just in things like *Our Sunday Visitor,* either. It's in fairly reputable places, in poets like Claudel, for example. Mary Daly quotes Gertrude von le Fort, who has some good things, but she's also got this idea that the glory of woman is to be veiled, not realizing what the real implication is. That's the worst part of it, that people who think they are helping women are often the ones who take this kind of thinking as their starting point. So you're finished before you even get started. It's like saying that the glory of the black man is to be in Harlem playing this wonderful jazz. It's crazy. "Pedestal peddlers" is the phrase that says this.

All this affects contemplative life. Being a *person* is what has to be emphasized. We have the backwash of this contemplative mystique here: we're cloistered, we have to be mysterious, we have to be passive and "beautiful souls." We're caught in a bind very much like yours. We've not been allowed to be persons. A contemplative is expected to be more dedicated than anybody else to an impersonal life.

We all have to fight against this. We need a whole new theological anthropology, a whole new understanding of what a human being is, what a woman is, what a man is.

The feminine mystique affects the theology of all religious life and of the vows, including the theology of chastity. If our theology is based on this erroneous view of the difference between the sexes, it's a false theology. It doesn't work and it will never work.

One thing you can do about it is realize that there have been people like Saint Teresa who did break through this mystique and then transcended it. How did they do this? Not by their own power but through God's power. The presence of grace breaking through this mystique gives us hope. With grace we can succeed. But we have to want to; we have to see the necessity of change and how essential it is to contemplative life that this mystique be broken up. Contemplative life is not just a feminine life, nor is it a passive life. It's the life of a fully developed human being. If the cloistered life is geared to developing some special feminine quality, it's anti-contemplative; it blocks the growth of a person. This is more than the development of aesthetic or intuitive qualities, or of a special tendency to prayer or a special tendency to love. Both women and men saints proposed to us as models were whole people. Everybody is both masculine and feminine.

Jung's psychology is useful here for the contemplative life. A man has to come to terms with the feminine in himself and a woman has to come to terms with the masculine in herself. The problem for religious is that celibacy isn't the normal way to do it; marriage is. Normally, a man would come to terms with the feminine in himself by a relationship with a woman: he accepts the woman as his other self in view of the feminine that's in himself. He is able to identify with the woman because he is to some extent feminine. Similarly, a woman develops by relating to a man.

For us, this integration can't be done in the same way, but it has to be done. We have to come to terms with the masculine and the feminine in ourselves. Marriage is not the only way in which this happens. There does have to be much more relating between the sexes so that we can make this kind of adjustment. In general, you can't isolate people and expect them to adjust to sexual reality all alone. That's a little like telling someone to fly when they have no wings. For this very reason it should be much more common for women and men to be getting together and discussing things and solving problems together and working out things together. We're capable of that.

Perhaps in the old days the sexual aspect of our life was more of a problem. I don't know. But today it's not that much of a problem, really. There's a great deal of shouting and hoopla about sex, but people are not greatly involved in sexual problems, most of which are artificial or misplaced. Many people do not know how to handle sex because of emotional hang-ups. Passion is not so strong that it can't be handled by the human being in ordinary circumstances. Sexuality is not overwhelming. But it is an important aspect of our life and we need to work out a genuinely creative adjustment. I think the program of married priests is symptomatic but not realistic. They're speaking out about a real issue, but I don't think the solution is for a lot of priests to get married. I think the solution is for priests *to be able* to get married if they want to, but I don't think large numbers of them really want to. Many priests think they have to marry now because there's a certain pressure to do that.

Whether a solution to the problem is for women to be priests, I don't know. I leave that to you to figure out. Mary Daly seems to think it's very important.

She thinks it's essential.

Right now, I don't see it. In her argument, Mary Daly is considering a masculine form of hierarchical setup and saying that women have to get into this place that men have made for themselves in the hierarchy. I don't think that at all. I think the whole thing needs to be changed, the whole idea of the priesthood has to be changed. I think we need to develop a whole new style of worship in which there is no need for one hierarchical person to have a big central place, a form of worship in which everyone is involved.

Rosemary Ruether has that in one of her essays. She talks about someone being called out from the group.

Something like that. Think of a woman all fixed up in a chasuble and a biretta! It's the men who thought up this ridiculous thing for themselves, and now the women have to have it. I think most women have enough sense to see through that. Mary Daly seems to fall into the category of women who want everything that men have, because "if men have it, women should have it." I think most women are smarter than that; they can see that a lot of what men are doing is just part of an artificial structure.

More games that people play.

Exactly. Many women see that there's no need for them to do that.

Zen: A Way of
Living Life Directly

I'm going to talk about Zen for a while. I've brought with
me a book by a German-Japanese Jesuit, Heinrich Dumoulin.
I know at least three Japanese Jesuits who are quite interested in Zen. This is a worthwhile book, not the last word by
any means, but good. This man has actually been in a Zen
monastery and gone through the training. Now instead of
the Spiritual Exercises, he gives his fellow Jesuits Zen retreats. They're as close to Saint John of the Cross as anything
can be. Frankly, I would say that Zen is nothing but John of
the Cross without the Christian theology. As far as the psychological aspect is concerned, that is, the complete
emptying of self, it's the same thing and the same approach.

When you talk about Zen, however, you immediately
run into a problem with all the Japanese cultural accretions
that are on top of it but are not Zen. Don't be misled by that.
Sooner or later you'll have nuns in your convents who want
to find out all about Zen and who may get wrong ideas because of this overlay.

We've had them already.

Zen can sound like a new gimmick, another answer to our
problems. We need a certain mentality to catch on to it, because it's almost too simple for us. Unless you're a simple
person or have a special gift, you'll go wrong on it instant-
ly. One of the first things you hear about is *zazen*, which
means sitting in meditation. But actually, in the Zen discipline itself, there's a formation you have to go through. As
soon as you arrive at the monastery, you're thrown out, or
there's no room.

Once you do get in, you're examined every year. If you fail, it's out the door, exactly the opposite of the way it is with us. Instead of trying to keep people, they try to get rid of them, because it's not a lifetime thing. A Zen monastery is strictly a place of training. There's a nucleus of people who are there for life, but they don't necessarily remain in one monastery. Even the master may move around to different places. A Zen monastery is like a college where you go for intensive training. A lot of Buddhists get this training and then go into business or teaching or other work. Many like to spend a couple of years learning to meditate; then they feel they're fitted for life. Some are trained for the priesthood. Then they get a little temple and officiate there and lead their own spiritual life there. Or they may just vegetate, just like on some other job! Some do become real Zen masters and teach others.

There are two large Japanese Zen sects. One is called *Rinzai,* and the other *Soto.* There isn't much difference between them. Soto-Zen puts more emphasis on just sitting in meditation; in a certain sense, it's like quietism. Actually, what they say is, "If you're just sitting there, you're doing it." Just stay there. Sit down, cross-legged; keep at it; be still. As long as you're doing that, you're doing well. And you don't have to do anything else. Just do that.

Now, of course, this is highly misleading from the start. Because what do you do there while you're just sitting? This is not exactly the approach of Rinzai-Zen, which is unique. Real *zazen* places a great deal of emphasis, not only on sitting in meditation, but on meditating *on a completely incomprehensible topic,* a topic you can't do anything with. This is much better, you have to focus on it and it's deliberately incomprehensible. There are five or six standard topics that you hear about. One of them is: If you clap two hands together, you get a sound we all know, but what is the sound of one hand clapping?

This is elementary student Zen. So you sit. You've got to work this out. You meditate on this and nothing else. Don't get any other ideas. Just solve this problem, then you can go to the next thing. So you sit, and sit, and sit some more. And every day or two, you go in to the Zen master and give him a solution to the problem. You say, "I've got something figured out." He looks at you and says, "Don't tell me that. Go back. Work this thing out. Stop kidding." So you go back and you think and think and think. When you really do this, after a while you're about ready to go crazy. But the master is merciless with you. And if you fall asleep, there's a fellow who comes around with a stick and hits you over the head to wake you up. You're sitting in a room with others, it's very intensive, eight hours a day. So you wake up and start again.

That stick would really make you get serious!

That's right. Really, the fellow's doing you a favor. You also have to thank him. And you have to make a deep bow.

Is that actually Zen, the clapping thing?

Yes, that's one of the standard *koans,* or questions.

Well, it wouldn't take two minutes to figure it out.

Well, what is it?

It's the air pressure against your . . .

Oh no, no, no! That's not it!

Now I'm clapping one hand. It sounds . . .

I don't hear anything.

This will have to be my subject matter for the day!

That can be your evening meditation. Really, there is no answer. Any kind of conceptual answer you give is wrong, so no matter how you figure it out, it's wrong.

Of course, there's a conceptual answer.

Not conceptual. But there's an existential answer. In other words. . . .

It's the sound there would have been if I had met the other obstacle that had gone off in the distance.

But you're reasoning. The point is, you can't reason it out. But there is an answer, and the answer is in you. There is some genuine answer that a person can come up with. It's an experience of some sort of inner truth that emerges as a result of grappling with this puzzle. These masters know how to interpret this. So one day you come to them and all of a sudden they say, "That's quite good. Keep working on that angle." After a while, if you're very honest, you get a big flash: "This whole thing is crazy." You will really know it's crazy. And you can go and say that to the master.

You have found out. Now you know. It's very easy to say it's nonsense. But to know it in your heart is different. It amounts to realizing that you don't have to solve this question. You have to realize absolutely, in the depths of your being, that there isn't a problem. Life does not consist in problems that have to be solved, most problems are illusory. This is what Zen is about. The machinery of it is simply to bring you to this particular point where you see and experience the fact that most problems are matters of self-deception. But you have to experience this.

You know how it is when we get into directing somebody. When people tell you they have a problem, it doesn't do any good to say that's all nonsense, because to them it's a crucial problem. Saying it's not a problem doesn't convince them; all you're doing by that is acknowledging that you don't experience the problem. They already know it's theirs. But they have to experience it as illusory. All the sweating and worrying simply help bring them to the point of experiencing the fact that they don't have to solve something. Most books don't tell you this about Zen. Or, if they do, it's not clear enough. So it's easy to misread what the sitting is about. People read books on Zen which have a lot of funny sayings and they want life to be funny sayings. This is nonsense. Or maybe they want to wear Japanese clothes or make Japanese gardens. This is okay, but it's not Zen. A book I recommend is called *Zen and the Art of Archery* by a

German named Herrigel. Have you seen it?

No, but I read about it in Erich Fromm's book The Art of Loving.

Fromm got interested in Zen through his contact with Suzuki, whom he knew quite well. I knew Suzuki, too. At first, we had a long written dialogue. Then we met. In a certain sense, he is my Zen master; he authenticated my understanding of Zen so that I could speak about it with a certain confidence.

Herrigel's book shows how Zen works in something that has nothing to do with what we would call spiritual. Zen is for ordinary life. It's not a method of contemplation. To interpret it as a method of attaining some kind of mystical experience is completely wrong. It's just a way of living. It's a way of confronting life without putting veils between ourselves and life itself.

When Herrigel was a professor in Tokyo, he wanted to find a teacher who would teach him the way to illumination. He was advised to go to a teacher who would instruct him on how to shoot a bow and arrow. So Herrigel goes to a master of archery, who hands him a bow and arrow and tells him to shoot at the target. Of course, he misses. The teacher says, "Now, for a while we'll just study how to hold the bow and arrow." So for two or three weeks, he just draws the bow. That's all. Just pull it back. But no, no, you're all wrong. You don't know how to draw the bow. Watch this. So the teacher keeps training him to pull the bow in a wholly natural fashion, almost unconsciously. One day the master goes away. And the fellow says, "I'm going to work this thing out while he's away." So he goes to the beach with his bow and arrow and works hard. "Now I've really got it. I'm going to show that guy I know how to shoot a bow and arrow." He goes back to the teacher and says, "Watch!" The teacher says, "Get out of here. You've completely ruined all we've done. I want nothing more to do with you." So the man goes away.

Finally, the master lets him come back on condition

that he start all over again from the beginning. He is furious and says, "Look, I'm not getting anywhere. I don't think you know what you're talking about." They're in the master's house and the master says, "Well, all right, turn out all the lights." They turn out the lights. The master picks up the bow, shoots five arrows, and hits the bull's-eye each time. So the fellow decides to stay with the teacher.

One day, all of a sudden, it happens. It's as if the bow and arrow shoot themselves and you just happen to be there. The point is: Learn to act in such a way that thought does not intervene between you and what you do. Just do the right thing without thinking about it. There is such a thing as being in contact with what the situation demands. You just meet it. But for this, you have to get rid of a lot of useless thinking, reasoning, explaining, and putting labels on things and saying, "It's like this," or "It has to be done like that."

Which is very much like John of the Cross. John applies directness to meditation. There's no problem with it if you just go ahead. There may be something you need to think about; well, think it out. But with something you want to do, like praying and meditating, just do it. Saint Benedict in his Rule has only this to say about prayer: If a monk wants to pray, let him pray. The only thing Benedict adds to that is: Don't let anybody disturb him. Which means, don't hammer and build a table in church at this time! Most of our trouble with prayer comes from the fact that we don't really want to pray. If I don't want to pray, I don't; admit it. But if I do want to, I do. If you want to do something, go ahead and do it. Get rid of all the convolutions between starting something and accomplishing it. We spend too much time trying to justify things to ourselves and everybody else. What is So-and-so going to think? Is this good theology? Is it according to ethics? or canon law? By the time you get around to doing something on this basis, you've used up all your energy thinking about how you're going to do it. Zen centers on getting yourself free so that you can just do something without having to go through a lot of rigmarole.

The same thing applies to psychotherapy. A psychotherapist who knew something about Zen just applied it to therapy. So now there's a Zen psychotherapy available. It's not for all sickness, but it's for the kind that most of us would get into, things like obsessions and hang-ups where you run up against some ordinary thing you just can't face; it's too much. You have to drive yourself to manage, so that every time this thing comes up, you have a crisis. A crisis is a psychological hang-up. Hallucinations fit in here, too.

There was a Buddhist nun who was seeing snakes, imaginary snakes. She went to a therapist, who gave her what's called "marina" therapy. It's a five-week program and you're hospitalized. The first week you're in an ordinary room, but with nothing. No books, no TV, and your meals are brought to you. After the first day the doctor comes in and says, "What are your symptoms? Have all the symptoms you want. You're all by yourself, no one is going to disturb you for a while." So the Buddhist nun who was seeing the snakes says, "What am I going to do? I can't read, I can't think." Just be there. Just live. And she asks, "What if the snakes come?" And the doctor says, "If the snakes come, observe them closely. Tell me how many there are, how big they are, what their markings are, how they look, how they act, what they do to you and so on. Just tell me everything about them." She says, "All right, Doctor, I'll do that." He goes away, leaving her to look at these snakes. Three or four days later he comes and asks her about them. She says, "As soon as I started looking at them, they disappeared."

The second week. People get tired just being in this room having symptoms; they want to do something productive. So they go out into the garden. They're allowed to do light work; they're back together in a common life. They have to observe everything they're dealing with. They have to pay attention to weeds and to little animals and to flowers, then come back and report on them. If they have symptoms, they have to bring them in, too. They have to experience the difference between a real weed and an imaginary symptom, and tell how they felt about each one, whether there was a difference or not. A week of that.

The third week it gets a little more complicated. They do heavier work, they have to observe more things, they talk about things more and write about them.

After five weeks, they're fine and they leave. You see how simple it is. There's no Oedipus complex; no "What did you do when you were three years old?" or "How did Mama spank you?" None of this. A lot of orthodox psychoanalysts criticize this method, but apparently it's good enough for ordinary hang-ups. It's simply letting people experience things the way they are without falsifying experience by labeling it beforehand. For something more serious, maybe you'd have to go through more. But for things like we've talked about, this therapy works very well.

What matters is getting people to avoid tampering all the time with their own experience of life. The need is to experience life directly. Don't mess with it; live it. If religious see Zen in that light and use it from that point of view, it's going to be good. But many of them don't. Too often people take something like this and make it an elaborate project, letting it mushroom in all directions. Instead of simplifying life, it complicates it. "How does a Zen person look at this flower? How would a Zen person handle a situation like this?" This is just a waste of time. It's non-Zen.

Of course, that's the kind of problem Zen clarifies. It sees things in a particular light, which reveals the problem spots. It alerts you. This wakeful attitude is very useful because spiritual life is much too abstract and too mental. We do too much figuring out, too much manipulating and analyzing, too much reflecting and watching ourselves do things. Anything that will get us out of all that is good.

I would certainly recommend this approach for contemplative houses in active orders. Many might also find "marina" therapy useful. For a great many people, being left alone in a room with nothing would do an enormous amount of good. Solitary confinement for a week. That's the way I make a retreat, only I don't do it in a room. I go out on a hill or into the woods and just do nothing for as long a time as possible. After a while I have to go back and do something. But I think this is the most obvious way to make a retreat. Sometimes I take a little book and read about three sentences in a week. I say the office and do the things I'm supposed to do. That's all.

This to me is absolutely the most helpful thing I can think of. It's what I did when I was out in California. I had every day free until evening, when we worked for about three hours. I had four days on the Pacific shore with no one in sight and nothing but water around. Doing absolutely nothing except sitting there watching the waves come in and the clouds piling up over the hills. Everybody should do this once in a while, every couple of months. For active orders, all you need is a place where people can do this. You don't need any other retreat. Simply a place to be alone and without obligations. There's nothing better. For some, it's a great struggle to do this because they feel guilty. If you're not congenitally lazy like me, for the first hour or so you begin to think, "Gee, I'm not doing anything."

But isn't that the highest activity?

Yes, it is.

Often we feel we have to prove ourselves. We don't know how to be content.

Exactly. So people don't always experience doing nothing as good. We're trained to think the opposite. If we're not constantly moving or doing, we feel there's something wrong. I should be praying or I should be meditating or making acts of faith. Anything.

In Zen, there's a great deal of emphasis on faith and doubt. Zen helps you resolve doubts, not theological but self-doubts. At certain points, we may have to go through a siege of doubts, not just about the existence of God, but in a way, much deeper doubts, about everything. This is very good. It's important in the spiritual life to go through a questioning of everything. Then we can let go of all these questions.

In other words, Zen living shows that all this questioning is useless. But you have to have questioned everything in order to see that there's no point in questioning anything. Because everything is unquestionable, it's right there. But we put questions in between what is there and ourselves. Underlying Zen is a great awareness of what reality is. It includes a respect that doesn't analyze but takes reality as it is. It helps us to be content with things as they are and go on from there.

I'd like to ask about this Jesuit who emphasizes the importance of a method.

Well, he's too hung up on method. You do have to go through a process, but it isn't necessarily sitting. He seems to give the idea that if you're not sitting there, you're not doing Zen seriously. That's not true. That's the thing I think is wrong with Soto-Zen, whereas Rinzai-Zen is different. To believe that Zen equals sitting neutralizes its whole meaning. Sitting may have a value, like our rules and the way we reassure ourselves that we've kept them. But it's not necessary.

Zen is very close to justification by faith. It's similar to what Luther went through with the religious life. A zealous Augustinian monk, Luther kept all the rules. Suddenly there came a time when the bottom dropped out of everything, and he really saw that you don't have to do this. Of course, the Catholics came along and said, "Aha, that's where he went wrong." That led us into a terrible hang-up for five hundred years. But it's true that you reach a point where you don't have to do all these things. You may or you may not, but you don't have to. If you do, it's not bad, there's nothing wrong with it. But don't base your security on observances.

That's like Saint Paul and the food offered to idols. Go ahead and eat it. However, if it's going to upset somebody, skip it. It's a matter of freedom. That's what all this is about.

It reminds me of the pearl of great price. When I was little, I thought how silly it would be to sell everything you had to get a pearl. Now it's so different.

For me, I see a boat that has been moored and then, all of a sudden, it's cut away and floats out to sea.

In our situation, I see that people have come to freedom just through living the life. For instance, we maybe no longer say, "Lord, that I may see," because it doesn't matter so much whether we see or not. We're free of that.

Right.

How can we introduce this to people in their formative years? Do they have to go through every problem and see that it's not necessary?

Each person is different. First of all, you look at yourself as honestly as you can. Then, when you're dealing with others, you sense whether this is something they have to go through or not. A lot of people just need to be told to get out of the nonsense. Often it's just imagination at work: they invent problems for you to solve. The first thing we have to do is to break any artificial relationship that exists. If we insist that people come to direction, somewhere along the line they'll make up something to say. That has to be broken.

To do that you have to abolish a large amount of direction. Just tell the young people, "Don't come unless you've really got something to say." Even then, they'll come. If it's important, you can listen and get all the angles and help them through the experience. But if it's something trumped up for getting attention, make that clear to them. Show them that they don't really want an answer, that they don't care even though they think they do. Much of this is simply being ourselves. You don't have to think about it. It just works that way. All of a sudden you know. We all experience that. It's ordinary.

I think the best way to help someone is by being yourself. This is the only way we influence others. Ordinarily, we don't accept a value unless we see it embodied in other people.

Exactly.

People usually know when you're genuine or not.

I think so. They may come with a problem, but a lot of it is just playing a little game. They come with a question and already know the answer. You tell them the answer and then they act like you told them something they didn't know, as if it were a revelation. In fact, all they want is to hear it from you, because they know you actually experience it. But there's a lot of flimflam about direction. Sometimes people write, asking me a lot of questions. I have to keep writing letters telling them I'm not in the guru business.

In my training years I sometimes felt guilty if I didn't have a lot of problems. It was like a deficiency.

It was part of the routine. There must have been some reason why the desert fathers encouraged new people to say whatever was on their minds. It was a special situation, of course. The novice lived with the hermit and there were just the two of them. Whatever the hermit did, the novice did. The hermit worked on baskets, the novice worked on baskets. The hermit said psalms, the novice said psalms. When the novice got an idea he said, "Father, you know, I just thought how nice it would be to convert the city of Alexandria." The hermit responded, "Shut up, you fool, and make your basket."

But the novice did get to choose the hermit.

Sure, and that makes a difference. It wasn't an official thing. It was a charismatic choice. It lasted for a year and that was it. The novice simply learned by doing what the older one did. Then he went to live on his own. No lifelong running to somebody else.

This is true about prayer, too, isn't it? You can learn something from others but, mostly, you just pray.

There's an idea around that says if you want to do something, you have to get all steamed up. It is a way of acting out our resistance, although we may not like to admit that we're resisting.

What do you do when you want to pray but it's just vacant?

Each of us has to discover that for ourselves. We have to know when we're asleep and when we're not.

I think we know when the wind catches the sails. But there can be a kind of cultic vacancy.

We know the difference because we've learned by experience that when you're vacant, you're vacant. You're half-asleep and in a semi-coma. The difference is very obvious to me because in community that's the way I always was. Meditation was a coma! By the grace of God it may have meant something. But as soon as I was on my own, it was different. Not that I was turned on, but it wasn't artificial for me anymore.

Other things were that way, too, like the evening chapter. I used to turn off immediately and stayed that way for the fifteen minutes it went on. I couldn't help it. There are many people this way. In choir, I used to feel sorry for one of my novices; he was absolutely punch-drunk. He was like a prizefighter hanging on to the ropes. And he looked like a drug addict. Now he has a simplified office and works well and is doing fine.

It made a great difference to me when we were able to go out on our own and pray where we wanted.

Nobody cares whether or not you're praying when you're on your own. It's up to you. In any of these compulsory situations, there can be a lot of hostility. Sleeping in choir is very often a hostile reaction. It's like sleeping during sermons, a way of saying, "I don't care about your sermon." It's an unconscious psychological defense.

Because if you're really interested in something, you're

not going to fall asleep.

Sure, provided you've had enough real sleep. The abbot used to get very upset when the monks slept in choir. He told them they had an obligation to say the office over again. I don't think they ever believed him, but it wasn't comfortable. These fellows were really sabotaging the office.

Back to the Zen masters. Do they really know if someone has experienced the reality of something?

They do if they're authentic. Here as elsewhere, there are "halfway" people. For instance, this question-and-answer thing we were talking about can get very systematic and falsified, vitiated as it gets spread around. Then none of it amounts to anything. There's no real illumination. Zen people admit that this can be a problem.

There are differences among Zen monasteries and between Zen masters. But there definitely are people who seem to have experienced some kind of enlightenment. These people are able to tell whether another is being authentically direct or not. They can tell whether people know something because they've figured it out intellectually, or whether it's the fruit of something coming from the center of their being. It's the same in our life. We can tell whether there's something deep going on or whether someone is just playing with an idea.

We verbalize and rationalize a lot. We're trained to do that by the kind of education we have. Sooner or later, in the life we live, everyone realizes you have to get below the surface of things. But there are some persons who don't, who just get stuck on the rational level. They stay with this reasoning type of meditation and won't let go of it, because they can't feel secure unless they're doing that.

Things need to get down "from the head into the heart." This is a more or less consecrated expression. If something doesn't really become second nature to a person, it remains just an idea. That goes, too, for things that are from the outside. Following social standards or somebody else's standards or the standards of external authority is alienating. A person may do that and it's all right. But it doesn't come from the heart. This is the case of many who keep all the rules but this compliance never means much. They're sincere and convinced. Yet, give them a chance and they'll do something that's completely contradictory, provided that it's not covered by a particular rule.

It's like playing the piano. When it comes from some place deep, a person just sits down and plays. Others will worry about their style and technique and what the teacher said. Again, it's a matter of just doing what you're doing.

Asceticism and Results

To put us on a little different footing, I'd like to start to-day with this good little book of Martin Buber's. It's called *The Way of Man According to the Teaching of Hasidism,* a collection of tales about Hasidic rabbis who are very holy. Everyone should know about them because they reveal a biblical kind of mysticism. These stories also give us the right kind of this-worldliness, as opposed to the wrong kind we all know. Hasidism itself is about genuine worldly mysticism. This means it contains the awareness that all things are God's good creation. God has, so to speak, put something of the divine goodness in everything. There are holy sparks in all created beings. The human task is to see these things and to liberate the divine sparks in creation by praise, love, and joy.

In this view, all creation is waiting for us to come along and liberate the divine element in it, so that everything becomes one great blaze of glory to God. There's nothing better for monks and contemplatives than this approach; this is how we need to look at creation. To look at it from a purely commercial point of view actually buries the spark a lot deeper. It does not liberate anything, and that's what's wrong with it. That approach simply uses things and refers nothing at all to God as source or end. It refers only to money. If you push this a little, you could say that it's an apocalyptic process. The Beast has got hold of everything and is using it for demonic glory. But we're interested in liberating the divine sparks, using all things for the love of God and seeing God in everything.

Buber tells a story about a rabbi who wanted to fast. The man was going to fast from Sabbath to Sabbath without any food or drink. He makes it till Thursday evening, when he gets very thirsty. He can't bear it any longer, so he goes to the well. But just as he gets there, he overcomes himself; he doesn't drink. Then he feels proud about this and thinks it would probably be better to overcome his pride and take a drink. When he goes to the well to overcome his pride, his thirst suddenly disappears. So he makes it until Saturday, having had this swing back and forth. Then he goes to report to the master, who takes one look at him and, before he can say anything, says, "Patchwork!"

Martin Buber then gives us a little meditation on this. He tells us that when he first heard the story he thought it was unfair. After all, the man did the job. He had to struggle and nearly lost, but he did succeed. Buber admits, however, that after a while he understood there was something wrong. Buber sees, and it's useful for us to see, that patchwork is the fruit of asceticism. If we try to do things ascetically, we may do them, but it usually ends up as patchwork. What we tend to do is to take the ascetic approach to everything—that is, we tend to think in terms of the will and self-conquest. If the emphasis is on self-conquest, we get patchwork.

This ties in with some notions on prayer. If prayer is something that we do, it's going to be patchwork, because I am a divided person, a divided being. So, in asceticism, I'm divided. Self-conquest is something I'm going to do; I've made up my mind to conquer myself. Then I must fight myself. I'm divided.

You may say, "Well, we're all divided. We just have to do this." But Buber says that actually what we need to do is first of all see that asceticism is completely secondary, and that asceticism isn't going to do the trick at all unless we are also supported by grace. The grace we need is the grace of unification. We have to wait until we sense that we're all of a piece before we try to do things like fasting for a whole week. One of the great things in the spiritual life and in monastic life is helping people realize when they've got everything together and are able to move.

This recognition is much more important than ascetic

self-discipline by itself. People need to have a *taste* for fasting and things of that kind. We might ask, How are these young people in the peace movement able to fast so much more than monks and nuns? They can go for three or four days with nothing. One thing, of course, is that they don't have a steady routine of being cut down to a rather low level of food the way we are. They can eat well most of the time, go out and get a good steak, so this means their bodies are better prepared for fasting.

But another very important factor is, these young people go into these things with a great deal of conviction. For example, if they are fasting on the steps of the Pentagon, they have somehow got themselves unified before they arrived there. They support one another; there's a kind of community spirit and almost a charismatic feeling that gets into them. This is good. We have lost that spirit because of the emphasis on asceticism, and a strong emphasis on individual asceticism. Each of us is left alone, more or less, to battle with ourselves and to wonder if we're not on trial in the eyes of others. If you get hungry and go for a piece of bread, you get worried that someone might see you. We've had some funny cases like that here, people who become obsessed with fear that they're going to collapse from hunger. So they store away a little snack. It doesn't have to be physical food, it might be a bunch of magazines. But something stored away, just in case. It's a bit silly, but it happens because people are not unified. It's important to be somehow together, of a piece, and united with others if we're going to fast.

It's the same thing in prayer. If I pray just because I think I ought to, or because I heard that it's a good thing to do, it's going to be patchwork. Then, when I ask how to pray, it's not going to help. I make a stab at it, I try a little Zen, it's going to be a mess. It will not really affect my life at all. This playing around with Zen is happening a lot. People hear about it, sit a little, pick up a few phrases, and feel better. But this does not unify their lives, and that's the purpose of Zen. It's supposed to get you so completely in one piece that it actually doesn't matter what you're doing. It's exactly the opposite of what people think. I mean, people think that Zen stresses getting away from everything and sitting in constant recollection. That may be useful, it's the ascetic side of it, the patchwork. But actually, Zen makes you see that you *don't* have to do that, it helps you to be unified so that whether you're praying or working or whatever you're doing, it doesn't make much difference. You don't have to care. You don't have to make this or that distinction. Zen is fundamentally against this dividing, it *overcomes* division.

What do you think about yoga exercises?

Some of them you have to watch a bit. There are two that I can't do anymore since my back operation. They're good because they loosen up all the muscles you breathe with. Body yoga is connected with breathing yoga; the two go together. These exercises look like tricks, but actually, each one has a purpose, and it's centered on the breath. All the bending and standing on your head help your breathing. And every once in a while, it's good for your body to experience things in reverse!

Certainly nothing makes me feel physically better than yoga exercises.

It does make you feel very good just to do some of these things. You can meditate while doing them, too.

One of our sisters is a real expert. She stands on her head about fifteen minutes every morning before meditation.

That's very relaxing. You get a different outlook, and it's fun seeing the world upside down. These various positions loosen you up. It would be good to do these yoga exercises for a half hour and then meditate for a half hour. Very healthy.

But what is the fundamental thing in karma yoga? Karma means "action" and karma yoga means simply doing your ordinary work, assuming it's human work, and not weird or strange or bad, so that it can be a way to unification. Your work is your yoga and it can lead to a sense of being one with God. (Let's use our Christian term here; it's not quite the same as the Hindu, but it suffices.) The work of a householder, the work of a tradesman, the work of a basketmaker, the work of a farmer, whatever the duties of your state of life, they can become a way to being unified. This is the normal approach of yoga. But everything depends on *how* you do it. You have to learn how to do your work in such a way that it leads you to complete enlightenment. Nothing else is necessary.

Basically, Hinduism says that your everyday work can lead you to union with God. No matter who you are, no matter how material the work is, it can unite you with God. This is exactly the opposite of what we tend to think the Hindus are saying. Of course, in Hinduism there are rituals and obligations, worship and prayer in the home, and morning and evening ablutions, and sacrifice—but work is the basic thing.

How are we going to do our work so that it's karma yoga? First, we have to understand that, behind this practice of yoga, there's a sense of the cosmic significance of all action. This brings us right up to modern thought, like that of Teilhard. The things that I do are not simply individual acts of mine. They are part of a universal complex of action; the whole world is at work. And in the Hindu concept, this is also the whole world at play. Above all, it's play. It's the dance of Shiva. It's the great game of God. It's like the child playing before God in that beautiful passage on wisdom that Proverbs 8 speaks of: "My delight is to be with the children of earth." This is a deeply Hindu, as well as a Christian, conception.

Hinduism sees, as we do, a manifestation of God in all that is happening in the world. God is manifesting the divine in play and art and dance and work—in everything. The Hindu idea is that I join in this manifesting of God that's going on. I work with God. There's this great thing going on and I am a little part of it. If I'm a shoemaker, fine, that's part of God's game, God's amusement. God wanted people to wear shoes! Or I'm cooking or making bread. It's all a part of God's work and God's play.

So, first of all, your own work is not overwhelmingly serious. It's never to be taken with the kind of seriousness that we usually give it because not that much depends on the results. In karma yoga, you work without desire and without attaching importance to the results. The work is part of a game which you do as well as you can, but without any desire to succeed and without any care about whether you get results or rewards. You leave that in God's hands. It's the equivalent of our doing it for the love of God, doing it purely for God's love.

So there is renunciation of the fruits of action. Why? Not because of some juridical, pure intention approach, but because of their idea of karma, which is a cause-and-effect idea. Everything you do has an effect, and the way you do it has an effect, so that if I am not working according to this yoga way, I'm doing myself harm. And every action I perform leaves a residue of some sort because of the way I do it. If I do it with a desire for results, then that will have an effect.

They are not talking about sin. They're just saying that if you do it in this way, it's going to have this effect. For example, if I work in an agitated, fearful way, I have to pay the price. There will be a result that I have to contend with. It's like saying if you go out and drink a bottle of whiskey, you're going to have a hangover the next day. That's just what happens. If you work in such a way that your work is a kind of drug, then you're going to have a hangover or a headache the next day. If your work is frenetic and demands a certain result, you may get the result. But there will be other consequences, too. You're going to suffer from doing it that way. All of us experience this. If we throw ourselves into something, looking for a special payoff for ourselves, emotional or otherwise, we know what happens. We know that it doesn't work out well. We're disappointed and frustrated. Much of this is unconscious. The way we work on our karma a lot of times is in dreams. We do a thing in the daytime, meaning to do it well, but we do it wrongly, our motives are overcharged, and we don't realize it. But that comes out in a dream. We get a kickback from what we've done.

Sometimes we get into a kind of tantrum. Or we get into a bind. Perhaps in dealing with other people, we're too dependent on a certain kind of reaction. Like someone with a musical talent who has to be prepared and has to be appreciated. In a situation like that, there's a lot of misplaced karma. Anyone who does things with a lot of concern about results, wanting praise and appreciation, will get other consequences. In this case, every time you are praised, you will need more. The principle about drugs applies to activity. Work can be a drug. A person who wants his work to turn him on may have that happen, but then it will have to turn him on more the next time. He keeps finding little ways of getting satisfaction out of his work; he exploits it.

Some knowledge of this karma yoga is absolutely essential for us. We're all quite busy doing many things. Often, we just learn the hard way. We find out that if we do certain things, we get socked between the eyes, or we get into a terrific tangle. Anybody who does anything in life soon finds out that you have to purify your intention, you have to do it with a certain amount of detachment. Otherwise it's disastrous.

The principle of karma yoga is good for us because we should be more conscious that, if we act in certain ways, we become tangled up in consequences and lose our freedom. It's a must that we be able to do things in such a way that we're not caught in a web of consequences that would be avoided if we were not attached to the results, if we were not demanding that the work give us a certain return. What this does is bind me to one of these illusory levels of existence. Usually, the one we get bound to is the mind. Our work done in a certain way lets loose a lot of thinking. You do something, and when you're through you go over and over it, telling yourself I should have done this, I should have said that. This can go on for hours. If, after you've done something during the day, you have to live it over two or three times before you go to sleep, your karma's off. You have not acted rightly. If you did it right, no matter how important or gripping it was, when you hit the bed you're out! If you find yourself lying awake at night going over things, consider which self you're tied up in. Usually it's your mind, because you think your mind is you. And you've been using your work to strengthen this ego-self that thinks and judges. If I identify my mind with my self, then my judgments and opinions are who I am. If you attack my opinions, I feel attacked. If you reject my opinions, you reject me; if you're right, I'm dead. If we look at this just a little bit straight, we can see that this is an illusory self.

This kind of experience vindicates the whole Hindu view. We have to become unbound. But this can't happen in one fell swoop. It takes a lot of time. There's always a tangle. You've got a hold on a string that's all snarled up and it's got to get unsnarled. It's like a rosary that gets tangled up and you have to get it untangled—it takes time. The way to unsnarl it is to start doing the thing right, and do it over and over again right; then it gradually gets unsnarled.

There's a lot to all this. It's good for everybody. This isn't for the highest mystics, it's for us. Anxiety over results is a large part of it. It's not only that I do a thing, but that I do it in such a way that I'm always thinking ahead. What's going to come from it? This kind of thinking is what we have to overcome. Just do what needs to be done. Let God take care of the results. You cut the whole thing in half immediately. If every time I'm doing something, half my energy is projected ahead to the results that are going to come, I'm working twice as hard as I need to. In any case, the results are not in my power; sometimes I can make my work come out the way I want, but a lot of the time I can't.

So forget about results. Don't put effort into thinking about them. Put all your effort into doing what you're doing. We can spend too much time on useless thinking.

Do you think our using these different teachings from the

East can make a difference in our health?

I don't know. Of course, we do know that the Japanese are now among the greatest consumers of tranquilizers.

Could it be that they are trying to absorb too much of our Western culture, and too fast?

I do think a lot of these people have gone overboard for Western culture. They're trying to be more Western than we are, and it's a complete dislocation. We've been building up to our kind of life for a long time. It's been going on at least since the fifteenth century. We've gone faster and faster and pushed harder and harder, until we are now really fouled up in our mind and in our body, wondering who we are and giving ourselves ulcers. Nine-tenths of the problems that we have in convents come from lack of yoga, from the lack of a balanced life, in which our body and our mind serve us. Instead of their serving us, we're using them in such a way that they block us. Then we act out our binds with our bodies or with our nerves. It's a lack of karma yoga. That's why it wouldn't hurt us if we could pick up some of this Hindu understanding and practice.

Is our problem a lack of yoga or a lack of unification?

Yoga is unification. That's what it means. It's connected with the Latin word *jugum,* which means "that which unifies, which joins." Besides letting go of the need for results, we also have to look out for the need to find pleasure in our work, the need for the work to be rewarding.

This opens up a whole new area, because there are many people now who demand that their work be rewarding. If I insist that my work be rewarding, that it mustn't be tedious or monotonous, I'm in trouble. If it always has to be something I like, I'm violating the basic rules of action because, again, I'm needing to be pleased. That's how I know I'm great. So I manipulate my work to make it more pleasant. But time after time it fails to become so. So I get more agitated about it, I fight with people about it, I make more demands about it, I go on strike about it and sabotage everything. You can see what happens. It's ridiculous to demand that work always be pleasurable, because work is not necessarily pleasing; sometimes it is, sometimes it isn't. If we're detached and simply pick up the job we have to do and go ahead and do it, it's usually fairly satisfying. Even jobs that are repugnant or dull or tedious tend to be quite satisfying, once we get right down to doing them.

One of the really beautiful things about our kind of life is that it does provide a certain amount of work that you don't choose and you wouldn't ordinarily choose for yourself. Then you do it and find it quite rewarding. But you don't do it for the reward. I'm thinking of some of the ordinary chores around the place. One of the routine jobs I get every once in a while comes from putting out a little magazine. You have to sort the pages. It's a simple, mechanical, routine sort of job. Of course, you have to put a lot of other things aside and it's a drag to get yourself down to the print shop. But I never realized that this would be one of the most satisfying parts of the whole thing, just standing there sorting pages. This happens when we just do what we have to do.

Acting in Freedom and Obedience

One of the problems we have as religious is the need for our actions to be perfect. When I need something to be just so, and the slightest mistake gets me all upset, this messes up my karma yoga. Always trying to be perfect is a professional hazard in our life. One of the worst places for this is in choir. This is where it really gets everybody! We want the tone to be just right, and we want everybody together, and no one off-key, and no one too loud. Choir can be absolutely ruined by this desire to have everything just so. It bothers some people so much that they just quit singing. Sometimes you can't get anything to happen; a bunch of people are on strike. This can be a very harassing situation in monastic life.

So the need for perfection is one we really must look out for. Obviously, this means doing things without worrying about whether they're perfect or not, knowing that generally they can't be. If they are, fine; if not, too bad.

How, then, are we supposed to do things? Once again, the Hindus have a whole attitude toward work which is very sane, very healthy and balanced. It's just the natural, spontaneous response to what has to be done. If a dinner has to be cooked, you cook it. If the dog needs a bath, you wash it. Whatever is called for, you do it. And you do what needs to be done in the way that it needs to be done. You forget about results and you don't worry whether it's perfect or not. You are progressing in union with God. This way of thinking is basic to anyone who has had training in religious life, and it's what we're all supposed to do. It's one of the staying elements in our life, the real ascetic tradition. Saint Benedict emphasizes ordinary work done like this.

When it comes to fasting, he speaks rather broadly, and he never has anything to say about concrete ascetic practices. What he does insist on is the kind of work we're talking about, work done as a way to God. He also insists on obedience, which we may have problems with.

Do you think that, without a special emphasis on work, lethargic people would become more passive?

Not necessarily. I think if they understand what we're saying, it would wake them up a bit, help them get into doing things.

But you do have to do your work in the best way you know how.

It doesn't have to be perfect, but it has to be right. You have to remember that we're living in the social context of twentieth-century America, where there's a great overemphasis on action. Production is what matters. So a lot of passive people in our life are, so to speak, permanently on strike against this situation. They may or may not know it. And perhaps they're right. But their passivity isn't right, it isn't doing them any good, and they may be neurotic. Basically, I think that if they once realized that they have something on their side, they would perhaps blossom out and work in a quiet and good way. Of course, there are always some people who want you to stand over them and tell them everything, and as soon as they've done the last thing you told them, they stop. And sort of wait.

What we need to get back to is an atmosphere in which things get done and they're seen in relation to what needs to be done. We've had a problem here of useless work, work that was given to you just so you could put in a certain number of hours every day. It was stupid work, dreamed up by somebody at the last moment because you *had* to be out there for three hours in the afternoon. Cutting down iron weeds used to be one of the famous ones. You wandered all over the field with a hoe, you whacked away, and then you looked at the view for ten minutes before whacking away some more. It was very bad for morale.

This reminds me of our famous story about the great impostor. The thing that really finished him was a very hot August afternoon and that kind of work. The weeds were about six feet high. And we had to go out with scythes and cut them down. He let it be known then that he wasn't going to stand any more of this nonsense. He was right next to me in choir, he was with me in everything. Later, he wrote an article about the place and told about someone exposing him in chapter for eating grapes when we were out picking grapes. I was the one!

I remember reading that. Grapes are almost the only thing that's mentioned about the monastery!

We don't have one iron weed left on our property. When we finished, we were on our hands and knees out in the yard, covered with mud.

Those things can be rough. Anyway, the basic and positive idea about karma yoga that you want to develop is that there's really only one who does anything that makes sense, and that's God. And it's God who knows what's going on. If I act in a detached, free, and conscientious way, then I'm working well, I'm acting as God's instrument. Then I'm fully in accord with the great work that I don't understand, contributing my little part. The real joy and reward that's supposed to come is a constant sense that I am God's instrument and a sense of gratitude for being that. If you see work in this way, then it becomes a source of peace and a real prayer.

Seen in this light, our work is a constant adoration of God, it's constant praise of God and constant love. A person doesn't have to do any more than live and act in this ordinary way in order to be perfectly united with God. Saint Teresa makes this very clear. This is fundamental Hindu and Christian tradition, and I think it's extremely useful. If we're going to have renewal, we have to incorporate this approach to work into our life and spirituality. It's not the whole story, but it's so healthy and basic that if we can get it back in, we're all right. We can't miss.

Could someone have the delusion that she had to be doing nothing in order to be a contemplative and then look down on others as being too active?

Yes, and if you think that doing something material disqualifies you for contemplative life, then you're practicing Platonism. That's the notion that to be engaged in material occupations is servile, the life of a slave. This is absolutely out of place in our life. But some of it got in. It was easy when you had lay brothers who did most of the manual work. They were the non-contemplatives, while the others in choir were praising God. This is completely false. Part of our trouble today is that people who are criticizing the contemplative life think it's supposed to be esoteric. Obviously, it isn't. But sometimes people defend the contemplative life on this basis. If there's excessive work, or if it's done for the wrong reason, yes. But there isn't anything wrong with work. It's perfectly good, and it's part of our prayer. All the saints who founded orders, like Benedict, Francis, and Teresa, knew this. To think otherwise is erroneous and un-Christian.

When we moved into an old house, we had to do a lot of cleaning. But two of the sisters wouldn't do a thing. They told me I was not contemplative because I was working.

Well, at least now it's more common for people to realize that the contemplative life doesn't consist in being turned on all the time and in having special experiences. Or to see that contemplation doesn't rule out getting your hands dirty.

There's also the opposite. If you're not working all the time, people tend to think you're lazy.

That's very true.

I've seen more of this than of the other.

Well, yes and no. It's about fifty-fifty. There is an overemphasis on work in American society. There's a certain element of the population that's obsessed with work, people who can't be happy unless they're always doing. Our heritage is being in a society where you just have to work like mad to get by. This was a pioneer country; people were moving in all directions, making piles of money, and the great thing was work. Some people are hung up on work, like some friends of mine. A lawyer friend I went to school with is typical. He just worked and worked, until one Saturday, working overtime in his office, he had a mild heart attack. He went to the hospital for a checkup. Before they could finish it, he was dead. People can drive themselves to that.

On the other hand, you give somebody a job in the monastery. They work 90 miles an hour to get it finished, so they can go and pray. They're looking for the payoff, the reward. It's much better just simply to do whatever you have to do. If you go along working quietly, you're praying all the time. It's important to get this balance back, and to realize that work done properly can't stop your praying. Work done properly is prayer. Properly: that means not having to get a bang out of it, not wanting it to be too perfect, doing it as an instrument of God. A deep mysticism is involved in that. It's not a mystique. It's mysticism, a way of being united with God. Our will may not be perfectly in accord with God's will. But the Hindu idea carries truth: God is the one who does the work through us.

But the work has to have a reality about it, too, doesn't it? One of our order's leaders thinks it might be best to buy things commercially, rather than make them, as we have done for centuries. But the General seemed to think that a certain corporate sense was achieved through making things together.

We used to try to do that here. It was understood that we had to be self-supporting in a very literal kind of way. To do everything ourselves was part of the Trappist mystique. It used to be a joke, you know, some of those shoes the brothers made. It was like walking with canal boats on your feet. Wheat doesn't grow very well in this area, but we'd try to grow it to make our own bread. You had to cut it and shock it and then the rain would come and you'd spread out the wheat to dry, then more rain, and the wheat was full of mildew. Then you made bread out of this. So we were eating bad bread for a year. One of the last years of Dom Frederic we had a very bad wheat crop. The bread was no good, the potatoes were no good, so we ate macaroni for a year. We had to buy the macaroni. But the whole thing was artificial. We do have to be realistic about the work.

In our monastery, some settle for a minimum of cleaning; others practically clean away the paint.

Sure, that can be an obsession. See, I'm preparing you for the hermitage tomorrow! I'm certainly not obsessed with cleaning. A certain amount of cleanliness is okay, but sometimes, once you start cleaning a place, there's just no end.

Don't you think Americans tend to be this way?

Sure, get disinfectant all over the place. Why don't you bring some up tomorrow?

I thought the floor looked pretty good last year.

I never look up at the ceiling, my eyes are always cast down in humble recollection. Listen, as long as the snakes aren't actually in the living room, I think we're okay. That's the one standard I have. As long as they stay in the woodshed and the outhouse, I'm content. It's when they come down the chimney that I begin to squirm. Only one thing ever woke me up at night, a flying squirrel. He was running around and I got up and found him, way back in the fireplace. I had a hard time getting him out.

Did it really fly?

It glides. It has a sort of membrane from one leg to the other, and it can take off from a branch or something and glide. Well, do we have any other questions about karma?

What about the question "Does it make any difference if you're a Catholic or not if there's so much good spirituality in all these other traditions?" We have a sister of Japanese descent, a convert from Buddhism. She had an operation and all the doctors flocked to her to question her minutely about this. Why did she enter the Church, since she already had all this spirituality?

People are rethinking what the Church is. Not that the doctrine of the Church is being changed. But what the body of Christ means. Insofar as theology is concerned, we know that the kingdom has come in Christ. This is the last age, and Christ is God with us. God has appeared in Christ, and the mystical body of Christ is the final manifestation of God on earth. And all are called to union with God in Christ.

If the Buddhist is really united with God, he is united with God in Christ, but he doesn't know it. It seems to me, from what I know of Buddhist converts, that their conversion consists in the realization that Christ is the real fulfillment to which Buddhism has been tending. There are innumerable converts from Buddhism to Christianity, most of them along these lines. When they realize that Christ is the fulfillment, they realize it in depth.

There was a beautiful article in the magazine of our order about a Trappistine nun in Belgium who was a Vietnamese Buddhist. She tells about her uncle, a Buddhist monk, about his sanctity and humility, and how serious he was about prayer and meditation. She also tells about herself, about how much the Church means to her, that it is something much more than Buddhism, and how important it was to her to discover it. I would not say that Buddhism is a natural religion, but rather a cosmic religion, whose basic reality is the metaphysical but impersonal ground of the cosmos.

Something that has to be explored in the relations between Catholicism and Buddhism is the fact that there's room for a personal understanding of what they call the "void." The ultimate for them is the void, emptiness. But it's not a negative emptiness, it's a positive emptiness which is fullness. There is a real place for a personal understanding of this. Some Buddhist philosophers today have said this, and they have equated the void with God. Suzuki, for example, talks about the void in a kind of trinitarian way, about intelligence coming forth from the void and about love and wisdom in the void. It gets to be startlingly close to the doctrine of the Trinity.

Apparently the Buddhists who have come into Catholicism have felt that this was the final flowering of what they had been looking for. It was in Buddhism but it was not explicit, and so the personal revelation of God was the final thing they needed. In itself, Buddhism is fine and peaceful and humble and a real simplification of life. But something was lacking. And what was lacking was this personal element, the relationship of a personal God.

These converts often seem to have a deeper appreciation for what this personal relationship to God means, because they go into it more deeply than most of us. We just go halfway. They don't get converted to that individual self of ours. When Buddhists become Christian, they're not just caught up into a rudimentary idea of the soul being saved by Christ. They find the Church an elaboration of Buddhism. It's not a deepening of their own Buddhism they come to, but a rethinking of it in personal terms. They retain their pure kind of consciousness; they don't develop an ego to be saved. They remain stripped of this. And it's within this deep emptiness that they see a personal relationship with God. If that's the case, they really have it made. That's ultimate.

I would say that as Christians we have the whole thing, too, but we don't appreciate it, and we don't know what it means. We've developed some things very well, some theology and liturgy far beyond anything the Buddhists have. But there are other things we haven't evaluated, and maybe these converts can bring with them into the Church what they have. Catholicism, ideally speaking, is the fulfillment of all these religions, it's what they all point to. Without the personal relationship that's revealed, the relationship of the Father in the Son through the Spirit, these religions remain incomplete. This is the final truth they all acquire. Unfortunately, this is what some of our more progressive people want to throw out, the whole teaching on the Trinity.

Some of the papers today seem bent on finding all the flaws in the Church and never looking at the pearl within. This bothers me very much, because it makes a bad impression on the young to suggest throwing everything overboard. We're quite close to the Taize brothers in Chicago, and we've also got wonderful friends among the Episcopalians. Recently, we had a Poor Clare abbess from their community visiting us and it was so painful that she couldn't receive Communion with us, after doing everything else with us. One of the Taize brothers visits the Blessed Sacrament and can hardly bring himself to leave. Why aren't these people in the Church?

There you have a special question. In a certain sense, these people are not making the final step. What they're doing is a greater witness to the Church at the present moment than their making the final step, because, right now, the reality of this division has to be seen. The whole point of Taize, for example, is that they are *not* Catholics. It's extremely important that they be as close as they are without becoming Catholic; otherwise, there is a tendency to obscure the meaning of the Church. The fact that people like that stay on the threshold is a witness to their sense of the reality of the Church. Simone Weil is another example. These people witness for the Church, and they're witnessing against the Church, in the sense that, historically, certain members of the Church are responsible for the division.

If these people were to come into the Church, it would be a glossing over of the realities of the division, because there are problems in the Catholic Church that we all know we're up against. Not taking the final step is a recognition of these problems and a way of saying that, if these difficulties are solved, then we can take the final step. With all their respect for the hierarchy, Taize is really saying, "As long as things are what they are juridically in the Catholic Church, we can't make that final step. We would be disloyal to the Reformation." The Reformation is something that has to be seen, no longer as a rebellion against the Church, but as something necessary for the Church. And the Catholic Church is finally beginning to realize this. So what Taize means is, when the Catholic Church finally and completely profits by the Reformation and the good of the Reformation can be brought back into the Church, then they will come in because that will be where they belong.

Would you please say something more about religious obedience?

The purpose of religious obedience is not to keep an institution grooving properly. It's to train us to become obedient to the Holy Spirit, to make us capable of obeying the Spirit. It's not a question of lifelong subservience to authority. We've messed up the whole idea of obedience by seeing it too much in the context of authority, or the institution. It has some validity in that context, but it's been greatly overdone. Obedience has also been tied up with a sort of alienation, the notion that we just simply obey and that's all that matters.

Obedience is meant to make a person supple, free from attachment to self-will. But it's not a matter of getting self-will broken by authority and thereby becoming holy. If you let authority break your will, you may just become a freak or a robot. Self-will is a problem and we have to renounce it, there's no question about that. In the death and resurrection of Christ, there is a completely valid and unchanging truth in the fact that we have to die to our own will, but not in the way in which it's been presented, as a sort of juridical and sometimes even systematic sadism. If a superior knew you didn't like to do something, that was what you had to do. There could even be a gloating. Such practice was sick and it's brought a great deal of discredit upon religious obedience.

Religious obedience is important because it liberates. When it liberates, it fulfills its function. It liberates if the Spirit makes us free. So it's possible to be free, even when there's abuse, if a person sees rightly. But it's necessary now, since the Council, to change the situation. There are times when one may not be totally passive under authority, when one must respectfully make known reasons for not being able to obey. Then see what authority says. In other words, put the issue on the table and discuss it.

But not just for the sake of not wanting to obey.

No, for the sake of a higher obedience. Take the question of conscientious objection today. This is a real issue. It's not just a matter of young people not wanting to be drafted. Maybe some don't have the best motives, but for many, the Vietnam War is a real problem of conscience. They see it as an immoral war because in the background there's Nazi Germany. And the fact that the Church in Nazi Germany did not protest, once the war got going. It protested before. But when Hitler cracked down, there was no more protest. And Hitler was overrunning Catholic Poland like a bulldozer. The bishops agreed that people had to go to war. Obeying constituted authority people went to war, with a few exceptions, like Franz Jagerstaetter. He was an amazing young man in an Austrian village who said the war was immoral and he wasn't going. The bishop told him he had to go, but he said, No, I've got to obey God. So they put him in jail and then they shot him.

For some people, the Vietnam War is definitely the same kind of problem. The bishops are saying, "You've been drafted, you've got to go. This is the law. President Johnson knows best." And they say, "I won't." Morally speaking, there's no problem about this, because they are prepared to accept the penalty of jail. They are only refusing to do what their conscience won't allow them to do. They are satisfying the law because the law says if you don't go to war, you go to jail. They are not flouting authority, it's not an act of rebellion. It's an act of civil disobedience which is perfectly orderly. A priest can't say that's wrong. In fact, the man who refuses to go to Vietnam and goes to jail instead may be really quite heroic, because he's being braver, in a certain sense, than some of the fellows who go without knowing why they're going.

Something like this might happen in religious life. If I were told to preach to you or tell you something I didn't believe in, I couldn't do it. Suppose a higher superior said I couldn't meet with you unless I told you this and that which would make you fall into line. I would not do that. That wouldn't be disobedience, though; it would be a choice.

Again, we have to be clear: obedience is meant to free us so that we can follow the Holy Spirit. We respect the authority of others and obey it, but we also have to follow our conscience.

Collaboration, Penance, Celibacy

It seems to me that one of your problems is the need for getting together. If you can get a conference of contemplative superiors started, you'll be all right. As long as you're divided, you're going to be in trouble. If you can get together and discover real problems, things will be a lot better. You've mentioned some local efforts, but they have the disadvantage that if the chancery doesn't like them, you're stuck. If you could get an intercommunity group going, and a bishops' commission to back you, you'd be in a good position to do what you need to do.

And if we can get our own chapters.

That's right. You don't have your own chapters!

The men discuss our problems but can't solve them. We're not even allowed representation.

The Cistercian nuns at least have their own chapter. But it's not really satisfactory because they can't act without the Abbot General. But at least they can meet and discuss together. Why can't four or five of you just visit one another at certain times?

There's one little phrase in the law that allows the bishop to give us permission to go outside. Once outside, we can make some decisions about what's to be done.

That's good. That's your loophole. Meet together as much as you can.

It's the only way we'll surface our problems. We met with our General; he took notes, then gave us lines along which to discuss these topics. It didn't go anywhere.

There's an active sister who's trying to encourage a mass meeting of contemplatives at Notre Dame as a way for the sisters in our communities to get some education. It's an effort to let them breathe fresh air, such as we're doing here.

That's good. Every little bit helps.

Is there an arrangement I could make to send two or three sisters here for a few days?

I don't see why not. Just clear it with the abbot. Our guest house is for families and it might be full in the summer. But in an off-season, I wouldn't foresee any problem. You just need to check with the abbot. I think it's something we ought to be able to do here. I want to help but I don't want to get caught. Sometimes people don't really understand your need and they wonder why I get involved with a conference like this. But meeting like this and having people here occasionally, in such a way that the community isn't disturbed, is very good.

We get caught up in the same rush as other people. Just to walk around these grounds is healing.

Everybody's got the same problem. Even in the hermitage, I have to draw the line at certain points. I think I'm going to be more or less available for two months, and during the next two months not see anyone. In your own communities, people need a chance to get completely away from everything. If you're constantly under this barrage of things, there's nothing you can do except get out of it from time to time. It's no longer possible to regulate life so that it's all peaceful. No matter how hard you try, you can't do it. There's bound to be pressure. But if you can get out from under the pressure, you're okay. If you live in the city, you have to look for a place that's really quiet, take a bus and go out into the country for a while. Just simply all get together and take off for the day.

This is unheard of! But it makes sense.

You have to do this in modern life, if you're in the city. If you're in the country, it's not so necessary. But city life has to include this. Everybody needs it. Even in New York, the poor can get on a subway and go to Coney Island. Keeping people cooped up is not healthy.

Could you tell us your reaction to the letter I sent you from our Father General, quoting the cardinal, saying that the essence of our life is obedience, chapter, and work?

I couldn't figure that out at all.

It's going to be a terrible instrument in the hands of people who want to use it to make life more oppressive.

You can say that the Trappists, who have the strictest chapter of faults of anybody, have completely rethought what it should be. Without making any point of it, change your chapter into a revision-of-life session. Get rid of all the formalities and ceremonies and have it completely informal and spontaneous. Let people speak honestly to one another, or develop a theme, nothing stiff. Of course, this could be much tougher than the old chapter. But it's good if people can agree and disagree in an amiable sort of way.

That requires a lot of discipline and charity.

Chapter should be interpreted as a process for mutual correction. That covers any current forms of correction that really work, like this mutual exchange in which everybody discusses things frankly. Certainly you can have the kind of session where everybody can respectfully disagree about things and discuss how this or that is to be done. The old rigid kind of chapter does more harm than good.

It was psychologically unsound and could be devastating, just the reverse of what it was meant to be. It could be too focused on little things, and even hypocritical.

We haven't abolished the chapter of faults, but there hasn't been one for about a year. There's a problem when you don't talk to people and don't really know what they're like. Some people are spontaneous but some aren't; some can sign easily and naturally, but some can't. We're much better off now.

What do you think is a contemporary pattern of penance for people entering our life today? Do we presume they know something about it when they enter?

No, because they don't. I think the question is What do they really need? Probably they don't need practices of mortification; these won't help them much. But they need to know that they have to turn completely to God. Penance is turning one's whole being toward God. All these other practices are just means of doing that. If I fast, it's in order that I can take on a different mentality, one that helps me pray easier. So you help people turn to God, to realize their need for God, their total dependence on God. You have to let their deep yes to God surface. Penance gets things out of the way so they can do this. It should be personal. Each one should be able to recognize what's an individual problem and understand the importance of penance from this angle.

Young people are never going to understand the old penances. There's no point in doing them. Somewhere along the line, in the novitiate, they should discover this and begin to understand. Usually, in our novitiate, they bring it up themselves, they ask about some penance they see others doing.

Often they don't seem to have a basic concept about love and communication and charity toward their neighbor. If we want this yes to God to surface, this yes that we can't make happen but can only indirectly influence, wouldn't it be important to help them find the lie in some things?

Yes, and also to see that, in fact, we do depend on a lot of little things that we don't need. Each one of us has to discover that fact and those things. We all have attachments that prevent us from getting down to realities. This is a subtle situation. We have to see clearly yet not fall into sweeping judgments about "everything worldly's got to go." Immediately, someone will think, My family's the worldliest thing I know! This is always a problem when each one has a special situation to cope with. If they want to fast, let them; that's not screwy, it's healthy. It's a normal kind of penance. Let them have the satisfaction of doing it with permission once in a while.

We discussed having some common penances but decided that each individual should observe fasting or do the practices according to her own judgment. It's more responsible.

That's a perfectly good system.

Community life itself involves a lot of penance. You can tell by the spirit in the community if things are okay.

We're in a building program right now and there's a lot of pressure, so we've stopped getting up at 12:30 a.m. for matins. Some want to continue it, however, after we're in the new house. Exposition night and day, too. But it's very hard.

Yes, that's rough. If people were getting enough sleep, it would be one thing. But some people don't sleep well, so you could have a lot of trouble. Even the Camaldolese monks who used to have that practice have abolished it. They try to get unbroken sleep for seven hours. Almost everyone agrees now that for contemplative community life, at least seven hours of sleep is best.

If we abrogate this, I worry about whether we're doing our part in the Church?

Do it the way we are: sleep from eight to three or nine to four, something like that. It works fairly well. Of course, it's not by the sun, it's too early. In the hermitage, I go to bed at nine and get up at four. The reason for getting up early is not to impress ourselves or other people but to enjoy those early hours. Sometimes I do stay up late at night and then sleep late in the morning. But when I do, I really miss the early morning. It's the best part of the day.

Those morning hours are very precious to us, too. We just go to breakfast on our own time.

If fasting is really effective, won't we miss it if it isn't there?

Well, you might. One of the things I really like to do is to fast on one meal a day, and take that meal at about three or four in the afternoon. Then the whole rest of the day is free and I can go out to the woods. You can afford to do that if you're eating decent food. And once in a while, it's profitable. You feel hungry when the ordinary dinner time comes around but the one meal is really all you need.

What about meat for everyone?

I think most people need it. You have to get protein from somewhere. I'm sure a lot of our food today doesn't have much value, it's not wholesome and natural, it's processed. Even the eggs taste different; you can taste the chemicals from the chicken feed. Often fruit juice isn't real, either. As for meat, I think we might as well take what we can get. As you said, let it be up to the individual, let people discover what's really useful for them.

Penance now means something that will loosen us up. You can be more yourself than you used to be.

Oh, definitely. It used to be that, by the middle of Lent, everyone here was so jumpy we could hardly live with each other. I can remember going into the office and it was like a madhouse. We almost had a riot. Fasting was extreme and it drove people to do crazy things. Now you can have bread or corn flakes, which makes sense. Without so much emphasis on fasting, life is simpler and I think we're actually eating less. Well, is there anything else before we stop?

Would you comment on virginity? The young people coming to us want to be virginal and they want to be consecrated to God. But the way some people emphasize this state as being higher, they can't accept.

What you're up against there are complications coming from the feminine mystique we talked about. There is a real freedom in simply not being involved in sex. I don't know how to explain it; it's just a more free kind of life. But, of course, sex is liberating, too, even though it can be oppressive in another way. It depends on the way we are made, like fasting or anything else. To be liberated from sex gives a certain relaxed sense. When you're involved in a sexual situation, you can get very caught up in it. Anybody who's ever been deeply in love knows what it's like. If it's too involved, there's real slavery, because you can't think of anything else. And there's no question of praying.

We're not talking here about a married relationship but about a passionate relationship. It takes all you've got. There's no time or energy for anything else. It seems to me that anyone who knows what that involves would be delighted to be released from it. To feel free again, to be able to pray if you want, to have a sense of being all one, are things we value in our life. Some people can give themselves to another in married life and still have something similar. But there are people called to this kind of freedom as a way of life, and they appreciate it. There is something telling them, This is for me, this is my choice.

I think our young sisters are saying that, but what they can't see is how this freedom is better than anything else.

I don't think it matters. I don't know if it's higher or not. It's better for me, but it's not better for everybody. There is a way of simply telling young people that the virginal life is worthwhile. Don't reject it. You might miss something very valuable that you are called to. I think this is what the Church is trying to say.

Virginity is a certain way of living with your body so that it isn't a hindrance to you. You are free to pray and study and work. There is also the question of all the cares of married life. Certainly, there are saintly married people. But I do think this whole wave that is running through the priesthood now, that you can't have personal fulfillment without marriage, is in for a shock, because you can.

But you can't just tell people this. And sometimes priests' training is purely on the intellectual level and nothing on the emotional.

Nobody has really told them what celibacy is all about. The other part of this, which I think is perfectly true, is that celibacy should be optional for the secular clergy. Because there is just no reason why not. If a priest wants to stay celibate, fine, but if not, there's no reason why he shouldn't be married, except for the historical reason that in the Latin Church it's always been connected with a state of good discipline and ecumenicity. So many priests have a drinking problem now. Of course, you don't know what they would do if they were married, either. There are no easy solutions to these problems. But there's a lot of hogwash involved in glorifying marriage. I think celibacy will have to become optional. Once it's optional, people will see more clearly. I think some priests get married to prove that they can. If they have the option, they won't need to do that. But if they don't have the option, many will probably marry.

Discussions like this pose a question for me about the relation between faith and theology. What is the difference?

I would say that theological debates are matters of opinion and that faith has nothing to do with opinion. Faith is the groundwork upon which theologies are developed.

Community:
The Place Where Christ Is Acting

We choose community because of its ends. People who want the same thing naturally gravitate in the same direction. Soon they meet up with each other. Let's suppose that all of a sudden the contemplative life is dissolved. You've got your community and I've got mine here. To be perfectly frank, I would probably end up in a rather different form of community, not in the sense of canonical form, but with a different group of friends. Let's suppose this place is closed tomorrow. In twelve hours I'm in Nicaragua on that island [Solentiname] with this ex-novice of mine, the married couple, the ten peasant families, and some intellectuals of Nicaragua, which is where I've been wanting to go for fifteen years. I would continue to live the way I'm living now. They've asked me to come down there.

You would be choosing community because of its relation to the end?

And because they're my friends.

Therefore, you're choosing community in itself, for its own sake.

Yes. I'm choosing community as the place where Christ is present and acting. And he has shown this to me by the fact that these are my friends. These are people I know. We have already discussed it and we feel it's a place where we could really do something.

Your communion with one another is immediately related to your choice of the manner in which you go to God.

181

Yes. And the kind of people we are. We're mostly writers and poets. We understand things very much the same way.

Let me go back into the vocation of this man who came here, the poet from Nicaragua, Ernesto Cardenal. I remember distinctly when his application came in. It was an average application from a Latin American. We don't quickly accept people from a long distance away: they come all the way here and in three days the whole thing blows and you have to pay their fare back home! I knew that the abbot didn't particularly want to take him, but something just said, "This is a great guy!" He came, and we got along fine.

Today he's one of the best poets in Latin America. He's a remarkable person and extremely humble. He's had an immense influence. He publishes in a lot of Latin American journals and is very well received, one of the few people who are respected as Catholics and as intellectuals from one end of the country to the other. He puts out a little mimeographed paper every two or three months and sends it around to various people. They like it. They see it as something good going on in this monastery. With no effort on his part, the paper gets quoted in intellectual magazines. He's simply being himself and there's a spontaneous radiation.

I feel that *that* is a place where something is really going on. If I had any further indication that it was God's will, it would be wonderful to be there. But people say, "No. You should be here." So, okay, fine. I'm old enough not to do anything drastic about it. Do you see what I mean about community in that way?

Yes, I do. What bothers me is that you're choosing community because of its . . .

Natural, human values. Partly.

For your need of it and its need of you.

Well, no. It's just that I want it. I like it. I like these people. It's like getting married. When a person gets married he doesn't sit down and say, "Well now, let's see. I'm thirty-two years old and it's about time that I settle down. So I'll open the phone book. What I need is a wife. This one's a woman. 'Hello. Are you thinking of getting married?'"

Suppose, now, you've chosen it. All right. Suddenly the situation changes completely. Your friends die or something happens. So where does that leave you with relation to the community?

By that time, you've got yourself another step along the ladder. You've got other involvements and other indications of where you should go next.

This thing will grow.

Sure, it will grow. There are connections. Right here, we've got a community going. For the last three days we have formed a little kind of community. Why are we here? There are all sorts of things that have brought us together.

Even though this was set up, to a certain extent it's a spontaneous thing. And the same thing with your going down to your friends. It's spontaneous. But our communities are poured into a mold. There are certain things that militate against their being spontaneous.

That's the other side of the question. To work it back the other way, then: of course, we are structured. And of course we are hemmed in. But then I would say, think in terms of the other possibility and refer that to what you've got, and see how much of it you can do.

We're changing some things here, but I still think we could be more fluid. There are lots of people that have left who might come back for a year once in a while, like a man in between jobs. Or maybe someone's just finished graduate work and wants to spend a year here before starting to teach. Lots of them could do that and people in the community would be delighted to have them back. Somebody that you remember from your novitiate days, fifteen years ago, lo and behold, is here again.

This whole admission of diversity into our way of life is

something new. It's getting away from the uniformity where everything always had to be the same. But what richness comes from thinking about diversity! I thought it was interesting that in Rome last week Father Heston, who is the moderator of our organization, advocated diversity in communities. He was talking about the religious habit, but he said that many sisters asked him why they can't do what priests have always done. And he answered, surprisingly, "I don't see why not." I think this applies to a lot of what you've been saying. Priests have always exchanged speakers in the monastery; sisters couldn't because they weren't priests. Or because they were women and weren't men. More and more it's clear that this is an artificial distinction.

I think you have to see now what's stopping you. Where *can* you move and where can't you? Are there points where, if you push a little, you'll find that it would work? You have to do that.

One thing that's come up with us: if there's a neighbor near the cloister who's in need, maybe sick, how far would you push a point about going out to help?

You would need to create a good community understanding of the situation. I would say the thing to do is *not* simply as a superior to tell a sister it's okay. Then you'd have people in the community who would say that this was really the end: "We've hit the bottom of the slide." What would be required? The community must see the possibility in the same light. If the community could come to see that this was something that they, as a community, owe to these people next door, and to see that this is the better thing to do, and that it's a real expression of their life, then you could begin to do it. *Then* if somebody objects, perhaps the bishop, you've got the community together. That puts a whole different tone on the issue. Whereas, if you do it before the community is ready and somebody denounces you, then you get all kinds of backlash.

I had to make a decision on this recently. There's a young fellow in eastern Kentucky who's on trial for sedition. I don't know the whole story, but I know he's trying to get out of the draft.

He's in the Peace Corps. Or Vista.

Something like that. Nothing at all subversive. But he was living in a prejudiced area and people didn't like him. He was helping the poor. So they put him on trial for sedition and he was condemned for "undermining the United States of America." One of the things against him was that he had the collected works of Thomas Merton! But he also had the collected works of Barry Goldwater. No discrimination! There's a priest in Louisville who said that we ought to give him sanctuary at Gethsemani, which the Council is now considering. Right now, he's at the local seminary. But I can see that neither the seminary nor our place can really give him sanctuary. I can't say, "Come here," because we've got people who subscribe to *The Wanderer* and love the John Birch Society. All of a sudden they'd find themselves in the newspaper with a man taking sanctuary, because some crazy hermit in the community invited him in! You can't do that. Sanctuary doesn't mean putting somebody in a magic building. The *community* has to give sanctuary. If the community agrees and understands, fine. Then if the press starts kicking and the Klan starts shooting the place up, everybody knows what it's about. People have their minds made up. They're willing either to go out and shoot back at the Klan, which would take us back to medieval monasticism, or to face the consequences.

Should you have a unanimous opinion on that?

Morally unanimous, as in the rule of Saint Benedict, the ones who are recognized as having mature judgment.

Next to our monastery there is a home for incurable people. They really don't have enough workers. I would have a little fear of the whole community making a decision to go over and help them because I think we'd be grabbed up immediately.

Of course, you're dealing with an institution there.

But if an individual sister wanted to do this, it would be okay.

Yes. But you've got a different case entirely with an institution; the need is there every day. If you start helping, you're sure to get caught. Your solution about the individual seems a good one, something the community will understand.

We had a similar situation here with a doctor in the community. A little while back he heard that many civilians in Vietnam were getting wounded and injured, with no medical help at all. Children have been burned with a blazing, phosphorescent chemical that's taking their skin off. They're just dumped some place in the hope that a doctor might get there in three weeks. So the doctor here felt he should volunteer to go to Vietnam. I told him to try to get permission. But he couldn't get it.

The community didn't enter into it much because the abbot didn't think he should go. Why? Because if he goes, another man will come in to the abbot and want to go to the Congo, or go build a monument for martyrs, or feel as if he's inspired or had a vision.

This is what you brought up earlier about the open-ended community where a person could be responsive to the call of the Holy Spirit. Not everyone in the house is going to be called out to do these forms of work. But I think the community as a whole has to learn not to give over their right to make decisions to someone outside the community. We're inclined to do that.

This is a big problem. This is why there's so much understandable resistance on the part of superiors to monks giving retreats in other monasteries and things like that. Obviously, as soon as you're in the market for something, you're going to be caught in endless routines, like going out every week to say Mass somewhere. I can just imagine what

my life would be like if I had to go around giving a lot of retreats. It's a wonderful thing to be in a place where no one
can come along and say, "You're on the mission band; go
out and preach."

It shouldn't be too difficult for communities to get a
new mentality and to understand that, while keeping ourselves free from these routine demands and maintaining our
autonomy, we could do a lot of one-shot things. You don't
have to commit yourself for a lifetime. The fact that you do
send somebody next door doesn't mean that you've always
got to provide. But we have to be careful not to run into a
moral obligation. When you're dealing with people who are
sick or really in trouble, you can't leave them once you've
started helping. You can't just bow out.

*What you're presupposing is that the community has a
firm grasp on the ends of the life and the essentials that
make it up. So that they won't make mistakes by commit-
ting themselves to something they can't carry through or
that will betray their fundamental commitment.*

Yes, that's right.

*But this has to be articulated. We can't just presume that
every individual has this understanding.*

No, it has to be clearly understood. It's a lot easier when you
have a good discussion. We had an interesting meeting in
our chapter one day. A couple of Taize monks from Chicago
were here. I was disappointed in our community that time.
It was the group that I have for a conference on Sunday
evening, about a third of the community and a good cross
section. The Taize monks just told what they were doing in
Chicago, being monks in the slums. We got a panic reaction
from about half a dozen of our people. They got up and felt
themselves called upon to make a long defense of cloistered
life, as if we were being attacked, just from the fact that
somebody said they're doing something different. One
monk gave a long rigmarole about serving "behind the
lines, and for every one out front it takes ten behind the

lines." I thought they'd have some new ideas, but it was the same old thing.

There's safeness and security there.

Exactly. What was so good was that the Taize people handled it very nicely. They weren't shocked. They were very tolerant. It was revealing, it showed what a difference there was. Here were these Protestant monks who have a real faith and who are living a life of trust. No falling back on an institution or a cloister wall to prove that they're right, no self-justification. How true the Protestants and Luther are on this point. We justify ourselves by a cloister wall, by going to choir, by monastic observances.

I think you have to create tension consciously in order for individuals to become persons. Our lives can be so narrow. You asked what we would do in a situation where we'd each be thrown back to make her own decision. We came up with nothing significant on that.

People in the community here now make more decisions, there's more leeway. One of the decisions that were thrown back into my hands was what to do about the invitations that come to me. I mean, a paid trip to Brazil! That's where the real sacrifice comes in. If the decision's made by somebody else, you don't even know it's happening. But now, all of a sudden, you yourself have to let these good things go by!

When you said earlier that there should be a certain freedom about these one-shot things, like the doctor wanting to go to Vietnam, are you saying that it's in the superior's hands to discern what the Spirit wants, or should it be the community who decides?

I think it should certainly be more in the community. Not only the community, but the superior and the community. It's very hard here because we're such a large group. In this case, I think the abbot could have brought in the Council. At least that much. It's a question about something charismatic, and more light might have come from a group looking at it.

Now, there are many angles to this. From a certain point of view, the abbot cut the thing off like that. Without knowing it, just by automatically doing that, he did actually obviate one very big difficulty. Soon after this, a number of Americans came back from Vietnam, people in voluntary social service that was not medical, and said that they were no longer going to do this because it was so ambiguous. It did involve support for something which to the people of Vietnam was a real burden, namely, our war effort. There are many people in Vietnam who regard our intervention as very destructive. They're not Vietcong, and they don't want to cooperate with us at all. Whether a doctor would have been accepted or not, I don't know. But it is something to consider.

That's the angle that always comes up with pacifism. The stand that I took in the last war, one I've always held as a normal Christian one, was that you don't kill. You can go in the medical service. But that's one of the arguments you run into with conscientious objectors: they say that even this is supporting the war. Of course, there are all sorts of ins and outs to that.

This question of where we are cooperating and where we're not is a very delicate one today. It seems to me that if we are really committed to following Christ and a special situation like this comes and you can't follow your conscience on it, then there's something wrong. If you are blocked, there's something the matter.

Wouldn't this be one of the ways that communities could grow? For instance, if this particular case could be put in front of them, with the person himself defending what he thinks is his call from God, then people would understand better that the issue is a matter of conscience. This process might strip away a lot of prejudices involved.

Exactly. We're a long way from being able to do that. Nothing can yet be discussed in community here. We just vote yes or no, and that's it. There is discussion in the Council, but this is private. The dialogue groups will express their opinion, but it doesn't go beyond that. At least, small group discussion is a way of getting trained in articulating opinions.

When the whole community is together, there's a lot of just sitting through boring sessions. This is the price that must be paid. It's the only way, but it's rough. People ramble, others just can't face the issues at all. The theological conferences have been impossible. And these are supposed to be the most mature members of the community.

Do you think the superior has to take more of a role in giving back problems to the people concerned? Sometimes the superior can be a scapegoat: if something goes wrong, "Let her settle it." I think if the superior points out that it isn't her problem, and people get the experience of dealing directly with others at the same time as they're getting the theory and understanding, this would be a real help. It's not enough to wait for everybody to get the theory first. A change of attitude is also required.

I think that's happening all along now. More and more people just have to do their own jobs. The last abbot did everything himself, he delegated nothing. How he humanly did it, I don't know. He had an old rolltop desk, and a big stack of letters for Masses would come in. He recorded all of that. Nobody else ever handled any money.

Why did he do this? Did he think he would strain the community?

Yes, I think he did. The general idea seemed to be that the less responsibility you have, the more you're free for contemplation. But it doesn't work that way. You have to have some responsibilities in order for the contemplative life to be serious. Very few people can live a contemplative life without any other responsibility whatever; that's a special thing. There's an idea around that someone in the community who has no particular job is the lucky one. But people can just be wasting time. How can they be contemplative unless they can be responsible?

Contemplative Reality and the Living Christ

We've talked about community, but I want to develop a little more the idea of reality, in terms of community. Reality is something you make. The kind of religious and theological reality that we are living is not something put away in cold storage somewhere that we can go and get a little bit out every once in a while. You don't go to the refrigerator and get out a little more mysticism or a little more religion. We're making the reality now. The reality of our vocation is not when you get back home and I get back to the hermitage. It's now or never. We may all be dead in ten minutes.

The book of Genesis is a tremendous book for contemplatives. But the first chapters, especially the creation narrative, are among the most crucial passages for contemplative life. Early Church writers knew this, too, of course.

Incidentally, I was very happy and edified and surprised and encouraged one time when I got into a dialogue with the Zen Buddhist Daisetz Suzuki, a marvelous old man. He is highly respected all over the world, an international figure and a great contemplative. We got into a written dialogue about contemplative life and Zen, which led to some discussion about original sin and the Fall.

I developed the idea in the way that the Fathers of the Church did. This may or may not be Scripture but it is in our tradition. The idea is that Adam was a contemplative before the Fall and that the essence of the Fall was a choice of a life of multiplicity over a life of unity. This may be Platonism and it may be all wet, but there's a certain psychological truth in it. Something built into our very nature lets us know

that there is a deep fidelity to the ground of our being, and
to a spiritual constitution in which what is unknown in us is
more real than what is known.

This ground and constitution is not existence, because
the deepest root of every one of us is one being. My being
and your being are the same. But my existence and your existence are different. There is one being for all of us which is
not God but is held in being by God's mercy and love. There
is such a thing as unity of being and this is also truth. This
is basic scholastic metaphysics, which no one dares even
mention anymore! But it is still germane to our kind of contemplative life. It is also germane to Zen.

What struck me about Suzuki was that he came back
with some fantastic ideas which could have come from Saint
Augustine, whom he's never read. Or from the other early
Church writers. It was exactly like that. Suzuki says that Zen
brings us back into this realm of straight being, away from
the realm of mere existence and activity. And that the purpose of Zen, which we mentioned here in passing, is simply
to get us detached from the notion that passing things are de-
finitive. We need to treat passing things as *non-definitive*.
They're provisional. Everything that happens to go by is all
right, it's real, but it's *provisional reality*. We deal with it in
perfect freedom because we are in contact with something
that we don't know. And we don't kid ourselves that we do
know. This is fundamental for the contemplative life.

Anything that is said about Adam in the Bible and in
commentaries on the Bible, in this patristic sense, is deeply
relevant for the contemplative life, because Adam is every
human being. What is said about Adam is said about what
is human in every one of us. In each of us there's a fallen
Adam and an unfallen Adam. The unfallen Adam has been
restored in Christ. We have the capacity to enter the
Paradise life, the life for which we were created.

One of the Muslim mystics writes that God said to
Adam, "Am I not your God?" and Adam answered, "Yes."
In Adam, all human creation answered yes to God. And we

all instinctively know this. There is something left in the depths of our being which is this yes to God. Whether this is simply a mythological way of saying it or not makes no difference. It is something we experience as basic to our being. If we reflect and think, we sense that the whole meaning of our life consists in this yes to God. Something in us wants to say this yes. By it, we acknowledge that God is all, and that from God, whom we praise and love and glorify, we receive everything. All life flows out of this deep yes to God.

One of the new commentators on Genesis has God coming to Adam after the Fall and asking, "Adam, where are you?" Early Church writers have similar passages which are very beautiful. We also live this. We experience in the contemplative life a manifestation of God, who asks us, "Where are you?" and we realize we're not around. In other words, this question is a way of God reminding us that we are not where we ought to be, which is right in God. This recurs all through our life. God keeps calling us back with words like these.

God speaking to Adam in Genesis gives us all kinds of typological situations for the contemplative life. Everything about the temptation and Fall is a pattern that we live through all the time, the pattern of our problems. Every problem involves a choice which, from something simple but rather difficult, we fall back into something complicated but relatively easy. Something that looks easier because it's complicated, because we can hide in it, is a complicated evasion rather than a simple confrontation. If we stop and think a little, meditate on how we function, how our life is, we see that there is an alternation between these two ways. We know there's no such thing as any of us always meeting the truth head-on. We just don't do it. But we do it sometimes, and that's good. We face up to the truth and then we fall back again into these complicated evasions. In a certain sense maybe we should. Like Adam, we hide. "Wait a little. Don't confront me just yet. Let me get myself together and figure out what I've got to do about this."

After God says to Adam, "Where are you?" our com-
mentator draws this conclusion: all reality hangs suspended
upon Adam's answer. That's the important fact. God comes
to us and it isn't just a question of answering by saying, "I'm
here," although that's a part of it. For Adam, in this situation, reality is the *admission of presence.* We make reality
insofar as we consent to be present to a situation.

The reason why this particular meeting is real is that we
are all here. This not only makes it a real situation but also a
saving situation. That doesn't mean we have to understand
all that's going on. We don't. We don't know what's going
on. But we're here. And this is where reality is happening for
us. It's enough if we just grasp this much. The rest will follow. We don't need to know. It's better that we don't know,
don't plan, don't know where it's going to lead.

When Adam is asked, "Where are you?" his very existence is a creative interpretation of God's word. God says,
"Where are you?" and there you are. If you're there when
God says, "Where are you?" that's the interpretation of
what God is saying. The interpretation of God's word,
"Where are you all now?," is that we're here. This is exegesis. Sitting here, we are an exegesis of the Gospel. This is a
creative interpretation not only of our own life but also of
the world. We can't interpret any more of the world than we
live in. Our part of the world at this moment in time is simply that we're here. And this is the world where the Vietnam
War is going on and we can't stop it. But we are here and we
know what we think about it. We are here living something
utterly other than the war. By being here and by being
aware of this truth, we are contributing to the next step.
We're not just sitting back and watching. We are making the
reality of religious life in America. Not by doing anything.
We're not making any decisions about it, we're not going to
pass a single law, we're not going to condemn or excommu-
nicate anybody, we're not going to start any new orders.
We're not going to do anything except just decide where we
stand and become more clear about it. That's enough.

That, I would say, is the heart of the contemplative life,

this recognition that you don't need any more than the real essentials. Everything else is froth. It doesn't matter. To be content with having met up with the essentials insofar as you can, that you know you can't do much more than that but you've done that, is central to our life. God will take care of the rest. We are "plugged in" and the current is coming through. That's about all we know how to do.

This same centering in on essentials is what we're doing in community. The main thing in community is to make sure that everybody is involved in it. If they're not, they're blocking it. If they're mad at it, if they're fighting it, that's all right: these are forms of involvement. But people have to be involved. There's no point in having contemplative communities in which everybody is simply playing it cool, and nobody has anything to do with anybody else, and everybody's passing the buck and nothing's happening. If each one is just getting by and has a little corner where things are fine and that's it and "Don't bother me," it's not community. If they're involved, however, and interested in each other and concerned about each other, then, even though they're not doing anything special or "getting anywhere," something is happening, something real. What's happening is theologically sound because it's taking place on a basis of faith and trust. There's no need to look for any other realities.

Suffering in the contemplative life or any religious life comes from the conviction that the action is someplace else. We think that what we do cannot possibly make any sense. Reality is always someplace else. The real meaning of the contemplative life is way up there on the twenty-fifth story and here we are down on the ground floor. We have no access to it. If only the Pope would come through with a document to put a tube to the twenty-fifth floor, we would be getting someplace. He won't do it. We're being kept from contact with the source of what would really make us happy because the Pope won't give us the key or the congregation won't open the sluice. But reality is not someplace else. It's here.

The other part of this reality, a basic thing we all need to recognize, is God's action. "Who is like unto God?" If

God can do everything without our doing any more than just sitting here and thinking together and being together, then everything is okay, God must be adequate. God doesn't need help, except our willingness to open ourselves to what's happening. This is a Muslim approach.

I'm deeply impregnated with Sufism. In Islam, one of the worst things that any human being can do is to say that there is an other besides the One, to act implicitly as if God needed a helper, as if God couldn't do what needs to be done.

This brings us to the real problem of the world of our time. It seems to me the issue is this: From a certain point of view, secular Christianity is saying, "Okay. God has turned us loose and left us to go along and make it by ourselves. But still, it is God who is doing it. So it's just fine to get along without a lot of religious activity and without all that religious superstructure. We're on our own."

But it doesn't work like that. Often it turns into exactly the opposite. We do have a problem in the New Testament with this whole secular structure, because there is more to it than just God and the world. There's a professional liar involved in it somewhere. What happens is the making of a whole structure of lies. It is not just a question of a good God and a neutral world which can be made good simply by referring it to God. In between is a structure of mendacity, of lies and false meaning. Except for the Mennonites and some far-out groups, contemporary theology is bypassing this problem completely. To face issues like nuclear war and race riots, and to try to account for them simply on the basis of sociological situations, isn't enough. The problem is much more complex. There is an enemy involved. The parable of the wheat and the tares puts it: "An enemy has done this." There is more than simply a structural defect.

There is a difference between truth and lies. The ultimate lie is that there is another God and that there is another meaning than what God has given. This lie gives us the idea that it is good to pursue or accept something that has absolutely no possibilities but looks as if it had possibilities.

Take the problem of sex in contemporary life, for example.

This huge effervescence of sex that's going on is not just immoral; it's a lie. People are buying a bad piece of goods. There's nothing whatever wrong with nature and sex, but sex is not a final answer. Some people see excessive sex as a kind of liberation. This is simply not true. Too much sex ends in death. A refusal of the Resurrection is implied in this attitude. People just do not see.

That's what's so pathetic about the hippie movement. These sweet, silly young people are running around talking about flower power and love and sex and fulfillment, and there's nothing to it. They've got an empty box. It's full of death, there's no life in it. All the talk about growth and joy means nothing. They just have a big box of death.

The only real answer to all this is the Resurrection. The only affirmation that makes sense to commit yourself to is the affirmation of the risen Christ. There is no other. Any Christian who gets involved in a whole series of answers that end up in another undertaker's parlor is simply being a fool. A person like that has no understanding of what Christian faith is really about.

This awareness is central to us because we are witnesses to life in the Resurrection. We're witnesses to God's truth, not because it is something that we figured out and not because it's something implicit in the structure of living organisms. All that's implicit in the structure of a living organism is that it replaces itself automatically, and that's the end of it. Witnessing to Christ's Resurrection is something different. It's based on a promise. God said it. You either believe it or you don't.

I remember one of my publishers coming here once. He has a Presbyterian background and comes from a very rich family. He started a publishing house when he was a sophomore at Harvard. His mother and aunts were all involved in spiritualism and communicating with the dead by table-tapping. He thinks there might be something to it. We were talking about Christianity and all I could say was "Well, it's the Resurrection. You either take it or leave it." He was quite shaken.

This is what it boils down to. Either Christ is risen or he isn't. If he isn't, as Saint Paul says, we're just a bunch of fools, the most to be pitied. On the other hand, we know we're not that crazy because we know from experience that when we commit ourselves to this faith, our life changes. Something happens to us which cannot be accounted for otherwise. Some people might say that it's a question of making yourself feel good. I don't know. But something does happen. This is the truth. This is where life is. This is central for us.

Contemplative life for us is a life centered on the Resurrection. Our contemplative life, as life for any other Christian, is Christ risen and living in us. There is no theological ground for any kind of contemplation except that it's the gift of Christ and his Spirit to us. Our life is the sharing of Christ's Spirit. Nothing else, unless you take it as something natural or psychological. Theologically, it's about the Resurrection and God's gift. That's what we're opening ourselves up to.

Gradually, over the ages, the Church has put something else in there. It's all legal and it's all right. But there is, nevertheless, the fact of power, which is worth paying attention to. The fact that, over time, we've built up the structure of an institution—institutions can be all right—which tells us that everything consists in being in good standing with this structure, can be very deadening. Of course, it's always said that the risen Christ is behind it. I would say we have to face the fact that, built into the good and well-meant elements in our structure, there is something of a lie. Something in the structure is not quite right. I think that the whole Church, one way or another, is becoming conscious of this. Certainly, Vatican II reflected a consciousness that everything is not right with the institution of the Church. Something has got into our structure which should not be there. We are all uneasy about this. Therefore, it's no longer a simple matter of being lined up with the structure. That is not enough to be right anymore.

We have to follow authority, but with a difference.

There is always a question of looking and seeing for yourself. "Am I in the truth?" You don't judge the authorities: they're just doing what they're trying to do. Can I follow them all the way? Is there a point where I may have to part company with them? That is what makes Christianity very difficult for us now. Before, it was simple—just follow. Put up and shut up, and you'll be all right. If the superior is wrong, it's the superior who's accountable to God; you're not. It's no longer that way. The superior may be accountable, but you are accountable, too. That makes it a lot tougher. It's no longer simple. Under the old system, the superior would say, "Maybe I'm wrong, but I'm doing my best." The subject would say, "Maybe the superior's wrong, but I'm exempt."

You do not judge authority, but you stop and think. Maybe if the authority is mistaken, I have to do something about it. At least, I have to discuss it. This brings up the question of the continuity of the past and the present. We cannot assume anymore that everything is a packet handed down from generation to generation. What I said earlier about making reality applies here: the reality of tradition is also something that we make. We don't just receive. The tradition of the contemplative life in America is being affected, for better or for worse, by what we are thinking and saying and doing here and now.

Maybe we are messing up contemplative life. I don't know. I hope what we are doing will be for the good. We are not dealing only with our own experience and mutual presence. The experience of people who have gone before us in our monasteries, their particular sufferings and frustrations, are all involved here. And the future is involved. The most intimate experiences of people whom we have known a little or perhaps a lot are also involved.

Will all this accumulated experience bear fruit? We can no longer say that it will, if we just reproduce what others did, if we just feel what they felt. It's going to bear fruit only if we are different from what they were. We owe it to them to be different in certain things and not to be different in other things. But we have to choose, it's not automatic. It's silly to forget the past because people then learned a lot of things for us, too. They learned that there are many things which need not be done. And they've gone through a lot that we certainly don't want to go through. If we remember these things, then we don't have to. Others have heard the word of God and they have responded in their particular way. They have set up things for our response, for our hearing, and we have to take advantage of that. But life is different for us. Catholic religious have no obligation to go through the modernist crisis again; it was over sixty years ago.

The reason they are doing it again is that they don't know it happened, it was so hushed up. Until Vatican II, many Catholics assumed there was still the problem of religion versus science, a problem that died in the nineteenth century. The modernist crisis was grappling, not with religion and science, but with religion and history. There was a whole new development. I think a lot of people are just facing that now. The French theologian Alfred Loisy was one of the big movers of the modernist movement; like us, he was struggling with adaptation to the modern world. He had to confront problems raised by the Protestant historian Harnack, who was very individualistic. Loisy also wrestled with the problem of tradition, using some of Cardinal Newman's ideas but without being as smart as Newman. He was interested in getting rid of the package view of tradition and, instead, treated tradition as a seed and Christianity as a living organism. Now this is all fine. We all know this. But there was a lot of trouble about it then. If you said these things at that time, you had to be very careful. It's a shame this wasn't all just put behind us, because that is no longer our problem.

There are other problems ahead now. Development and adaptation in religious life are being thought out in modernist terms, and that's too bad. All the press coverage about renewal is sixty years behind the times. The critics are once again thinking in terms of freedom from authority and tradition in the old sense. There is a need for real authority—but it has to be of a different kind. Just when we are getting a little free from the wrong kind of authority, some people are trying to find a moralistic need for a "right concept" of authority. This is useless.

The reality of tradition is Christ himself. The meaning of "Christ is risen and Christ lives" is that Christ has *really* risen and lives in us now. It's a question of the reality of a tradition that is *alive*. It's a matter of Christ actually being and living here and now in us.

If we let the risen Christ live in us, then we can go ahead with confidence, very sure that we're walking in the name of the Father and of the Son and of the Holy Spirit. Amen.

Amen!

Appendix

Loretto and Gethsemani

Editor's Note: *In the spring of 1962, Merton wrote the following reflection for the Sisters of Loretto, who were celebrating the 150th anniversary of the founding of their congregation. While it highlights connections between Loretto and Gethsemani, its central message of the Cross is for all who "struggle to keep awake under the moonlit olive trees."*

We are not only neighbors in a Kentucky valley that is still lonely, but we are equally children of exile and of revolution. Perhaps this is a good reason why we are both hidden in the same mystery of Our Lady's Sorrow and Solitude in the Lord's Passion. We cannot understand our vocation except in the light of that solitude and that love, in which we are as inextricably one as the bones of the founders of two Gethsemanis in one grave: the first Lorettine nuns who dedicated the place to Mary and the first Breton Trappists who took it over from them. All who were buried in back of the Dant house, the log cabin that was the first Gethsemani in Kentucky, are now together under the nameless concrete cross behind the abbey church. Their anonymity, their community in death, is eloquent, but probably most of us have ceased to notice it, or have never even been aware of it in the first place.

Father Nerinckx was born in 1761 in Brabant, a region [of Belgium] which was perhaps more fertile in Cistercian saints than any other. He fled to America from the revolutionary armies of France, and from the constitutional oath which he could not take. He was appointed to Kentucky, where Father Badin was the only priest. He started West in

1805 with the first Trappist colony, Dom Urban Guillet's fugitives from Napoleonic France. But Father Nerinckx moved faster and reached Kentucky before them. He helped them get settled in Holy Cross and Casey Creek. He spent days and nights in their monastery when he was able. He wanted to become one of them. He had the same rigid, austere, uncompromising, and generally unsmiling spirit. Like them, he saw all things in black and white; it was simpler that way, though not always more revealing. He never managed to obtain permission to join the monks. If he had done so, he would presently have left Kentucky with them forever, and returned to France. Instead of that he built Saint Stephen's and helped to establish a seminary there. On that same site the Loretto Motherhouse now stands.

Father Nerinckx founded one of the first completely American congregations of sisters. The nuns were Catholic pioneers who had come from Maryland to Nelson County and who started a school in an abandoned, broken-down log cabin in 1812. They refused to let sisters be called from Europe to give shape to the new institute. They knew how to grow and acquire the spirit willed by God, under the guidance of their director. The rugged simplicity of Loretto still has a healthy, early American quality about it. One does not sense there too many of the rigid and deadening formalities which many other congregations have brought from across the ocean.

It was five years after the Congregation of Loretto came into existence that the Dant family gave them a house on Pottinger's Creek, which had long been a mission station. In 1818 the nuns started a school there and called it Gethsemani. They operated this school for thirty years, and then a Trappist monk from France, a Father Paulinus of the Abbey of Melleray, appeared in the country looking for land. It was once again a year of revolution, and the Trappists of Melleray, near Nantes, were threatened with expulsion. Father Paulinus agreed to buy this farm, and at the end of 1848 a colony of monks took it over from the sisters. They settled down to till the fields in silence. It is not recorded that they were very often aware of the existence of nearby Loretto. But I suppose that from the earliest days there have occasionally been some Lorettines seen in the back of our church. (Pardon me, not seen. We like to believe that we never look.)

Quietly, efficiently, the Lorettines began to spread out over the country, westward and southward. Already before the end of the nineteenth century, they had raised many of the ponderous brick academies fashionable at that time. The Trappists stayed in their valley. They were busy keeping body and soul together. They, too, had an academy. They even started a congregation of nuns of their own, which got away from them in a storm of juridical red tape and drifted to Indiana. And after that the boys' school burned down and the Trappists went out of business as educators. Loretto continued to grow and to prosper. The Trappists continued to exist.

Finally, at the end of the Second World War, Gethsemani stirred to life. Two Cistercian foundations went south, two went west, and one went north. No one has yet explained why, suddenly, so many Americans wanted to become Cistercians. Such things do not need to be explained. In any case, explanations are misleading. There are things about Gethsemani that cannot be put into any words whatever; still less can they be comprehensively published for the edification of multitudes.

There is something about Gethsemani that has nothing to communicate to multitudes, and I find it also at Loretto. It is a secret that reveals itself only partially even to those who live for a long time in our valley.

I suppose I will give scandal if I say it is a quiet mixture of wisdom and madness, a triumph of hope over despair. But we have both descended from ancestors who died accomplishing the impossible. Or rather, from people who accepted as perfectly normal the incongruity and solitude which are the lot of the pioneer. Now we are safer than they, richer, more comfortable, better cared for, secure. But when I say there is madness in the old walls of our houses, I mean a wise madness that still, for all the public approval we have received from "the world," persists in a half-ironic suspicion that all is not well with the world, and that we cannot be altogether part of it. This I know is the thing I must not say. We are, of course, engagés. We are in the world of our time, no doubt about that. We are in it to save it. Yet we still have to save ourselves from it, for unless we have a foothold that is not of this world, we will go down with it, and drag no one to safety.

You are daughters, not of the American, but of the French Revolution. Hence daughters not on Park Avenue but in this hot valley, and at the foot of the Cross. I think we have to remember that if we pray for the people on Park Avenue, no less than for those on Skid Row, we are not praying for Park Avenue or for Skid Row as such. We are not satisfied with the status quo, no matter how plush it may be for very many. The point of our striving is not that the world should be rich, but that it should be Christian. And in a time like ours, at least in this country, there is always the satanic temptation to identify holiness with prosperity. It has become an old habit of our rich nation to turn the beatitudes inside out and to assume that we must indeed be meek because we have inherited the land. Especially somebody else's land. In a word, we have reaped the harvest sown by the pioneers, and it is enormous. Yet we have assumed that because they were courageous they had, perhaps, all the other virtues together with fortitude; and that because we are the richest people in the world we are also the most righteous.

It is true that our adversaries have the luxury of proclaiming themselves godless and they can dispense from asking themselves questions like these. We who are consecrated to Christ retain the dubious privilege of acting as a kind of conscience in a confused and increasingly conscienceless world of pragmatism and laissez-faire. In this society of ours we must frankly admit a tragic intellectual and moral incoherence where the only universal principle is "whatever works is right." Then when things stop working, all is wrong. Our Christian ethic is not based on any such relativism. Our standards rise above the fluctuations and accidents of sociological change.

In Christ, God has revealed to us divine love, divine truth, and the divine will; and we have accepted this revelation by freely choosing to be loyal to Christ and his Church in prosperity and adversity, war and peace, in freedom or in prison. This loyalty is the price and guarantee of the only true freedom, and it is on this ideal that the culture of the Christian West has been built Now that the West has rejected this ideal, and forfeited its spiritual inheritance, the task of those consecrated to God in religion becomes increasingly difficult. The difficulty itself is, then, essential to our vocation. Only by accepting the fact that we are in some sense exiles at odds with materialism, commercialism, and secularism can we begin to be fully faithful to Christ. We must sometimes be resolutely unfashionable, both in morals and in intelligence. This does not mean a cult of anachronism; on the contrary, it is a kind of dissent which is necessary for genuine growth. And Christian dissent is all the more essential as we enter what C. S. Lewis has called the *post-Christian* era.

Let us be persuaded that we can dissent without at the same time becoming fanatics, but that our first duty is to preserve the purity of our faith.

There is nothing more positive, more creative than the faith by which the Creator of all dwells and acts in our hearts. And yet, as we know from our own past history, the ideal of "keeping the faith" can sometimes dwindle into something very negative, resentful, and obtuse: a mere "no" to everything that we do not agree with. We can no longer afford to barricade ourselves in our Catholic environment and regard it as a little smug fortress of security in a world of pagans. Now most of all we are obliged by our faith and by our love of truth to commit ourselves humbly and completely, not only to the message of Christ, but also to all that is valid in human culture and civilization, for this, too, is his by right. Not only is it something that we must salvage for Christ, but more, it is not unconnected with our own salvation. If the Lord of all took flesh and sanctified all nature, restoring it to the Father by his Resurrection, we, too, have our work to do in extending the power of the Resurrection to the whole world of our time by our prayer, our thought, our work, and our whole life. Nothing so effectively prevents this as the division, the discontinuity of spiritual lives that place God and prayer in one compartment, work and apostolate in another, as if prayer and work were somehow opposed. The Cross is the sign of contradiction, but also and above all the sign of reconciliation. It reminds us of the contradictions within ourselves, and within our society, only in order to resolve them all in unity in love of the Saviour. Unity is a sign of strength and spiritual health. This unity in Christ is the true secret of our Christian and religious vocations, whether our lives be active or contemplative.

False unity is the work of force. It is violently imposed on divided entities which stubbornly refuse to be one. True unity is the work of love. It is the free union of beings that spontaneously seek to be one in the truth, preserving and elevating their separate selves by self-transcendence. False unity strives to assert itself by the denial of obstacles. True unity admits the presence of obstacles and of divisions in order to overcome both by humility and sacrifice.

Here, in facing contradiction, we can hope for grace from God that will produce a unity and a peace "which the world cannot give."

It is clear, then, that our vocation to love the truth is also a vocation to love the Cross. Our lives therefore are to be led purely and simply under a sign of contradiction. This may sometimes create much anguish both for ourselves and for those who come in contact with us. But this anguish is our inheritance. It is our substitute for the solitude and insecurity of the pioneer. The Christian life is not an enclosed garden in which we can sit at ease, protected by the love of God. It is, alas, a wilderness into which we can be led by the Spirit in order to be tempted by the Devil.

Or, a garden where, while Christ sweats blood in an agony beyond our comprehension, we "struggle to keep awake under the moonlit olive trees."